GLOBETROTTER

Travel

CANARY ISLANDS

ANDY GRAVETTE

NEW HOLLAND

NEW HOLLAND

> ★★★ Highly recommended
> ★★ Recommended
> ★ See if you can

This edition first published in 2000
by New Holland Publishers (UK) Ltd
London • Cape Town • Sydney • Auckland
First edition published in 1996
10 9 8 7 6 5 4 3 2 1

24 Nutford Place
London W1H 6DQ
United Kingdom

80 McKenzie Street
Cape Town 8001
South Africa

14 Aquatic Drive
Frenchs Forest, NSW 2086
Australia

218 Lake Road
Northcote, Auckland
New Zealand

Distributed in the USA by
The Globe Pequot Press
Connecticut

Copyright © 2000 in text: Andy Gravette
Copyright © 2000 in maps: Globetrotter Travel Maps
Copyright © 2000 in photographs:
Individual photographers as credited (right)
Copyright © 2000 New Holland (Publishers) Ltd

All rights reserved. No part of this publication
may be reproduced, stored in a retrieval system
or transmitted, in any form or by any means,
electronic, mechanical, photocopying, recording
or otherwise, without the prior written permission
of the publishers and copyright holders.

ISBN 1 85974 531 8

Although every effort has been made to ensure
accuracy of facts, telephone and fax numbers in this
book, the publishers will not be held responsible for
changes that occur at the time of going to press.

Commissioning Editor: Tim Jollands
Manager Globetrotter Maps: John Loubser
Editors: Thea Grobbelaar, Susannah Coucher, Sara Harper
Picture Researcher: Emily Hedges
Design and DTP: Kathryn Fotheringham
Cartographer: Karen Bayley
Compiler/Verifier: Elaine Fick
Reproduction by Hirt & Carter (Pty) Ltd, Cape Town
Printed and bound in Hong Kong by Sing Cheong
Printing Co. Ltd.

Photographic Credits:
Jeanetta Baker/PhotoBank, cover; **A. Bartel/
Fotoccompli**, pages 98, 101; **Juan M. Castro**, pages
105, 106; **Abbie Enock/Travel Ink**, pages 22, 52, 55,
61, 62 (top right); **Robert Frerck** (*RHPL*), pages 14,
15 (bottom), 17, 24 (left), 27, 28 (bottom), 43, 66, 71,
77, 93, 95; **Andy Gravette**, pages 21, 88, 110;
G. Hellier (*RHPL*), pages 6, 103; *Courtesy of* **The
Mansell Collection**, page 12; **Paul Murphy**, pages
10, 15 (top), 18, 19, 20, 23, 25, 28 (top), 29 (bottom),
33, 37, 58, 59 (top), 60, 69 (top and bottom), 70, 74,
76, 85 (left and right), 87, 89, 109, 117, 118, 120;
Paul Phillips (*RHPL*), page 40; **Mike L. Pollitt**,
page 49; **Rolf Richardson** (*RHPL*), pages 16, 26, 108;
Robert Harding Picture Library (*RHPL*), pages 7, 9,
13, 24 (right), 29 (top), 30, 34, 35, 36, 44, 46, 47 (top
and bottom), 57, 59 (bottom), 62 (top left), 63, 82, 90,
91, 94, 112, 114, 115, 116, 119; **Robin Scagell** (*RHPL*),
pages 104, 107; **Bildagentur Schuster** (*RHPL*), pages
8, 48; **Ray Ward**, title page; **Geoff Williamson**
(*RHPL*), pages 72, 92; **Trevor Wood** (*RHPL*), pages
73, 75, 78, 79.

Cover: *The colourful fishing boat harbour of Puerto
de Mogán, Gran Canaria.*
Title page: *Women in costume for Thanksgiving
at Betancuria, Fuerteventura, wearing the island's
characteristic pointed hat.*

CONTENTS

**1. Introducing
the Canary Islands 5**
The Land 6
History in Brief 10
Government and Economy 15
The People 17

2. Las Palmas 31
Vegueta Quarter 33
Triana District 35
Las Palmas Shopping 37

3. Gran Canaria 41
The Coastal Resorts 42
A Coastal Tour 43
A Mountain Tour 46

4. Fuerteventura 53
Puerto del Rosario 55
North from Puerto
del Rosario 56
West from Puerto
del Rosario 59
South from Puerto
del Rosario 61

5. Lanzarote 67
Arrecife 69
Timanfaya National Park 71
Teguise 75
Around the North 76
La Graciosa 78

6. Tenerife 83
Santa Cruz de Tenerife 84
Inland from Santa Cruz 88
The Coast 93

7. La Palma 99
Santa Cruz de La Palma 100
Touring the Island 103

**8. La Gomera and
El Hierro 113**
San Sebastián
de La Gomera 115
El Hierro 118

Travel Tips 122

Index 127

1
Introducing the Canary Islands

Basking in glorious year-round sunshine and surrounded by the aquamarine water of the Atlantic Ocean, each of the seven major Canary islands has its own unique charm. The majority of tourists flock to the endless strings of white sandy beaches, to enjoy the fabulous watersports and dance the night away in the high-energy clubs on Gran Canaria and Tenerife. Yet within minutes of the coast, even the most popular islands have a wealth of astonishing natural beauty, almost untouched by the modern world.

Gran Canaria is an exhilarating blend of old and new, backed by breathtaking scenery and with a cosmopolitan capital. **Fuerteventura** has spectacular sandy beaches with some of the best windsurfing conditions in the world. **Lanzarote's** haunting beauty is encapsulated in the eerie lunar landscape of Timanfaya National Park. The snow-capped peak of Mount Teide looms over **Tenerife's** lush vegetation. One of the world's largest volcanic craters dominates peaceful **La Palma**; **La Gomera** and **El Hierro** are even more tranquil. It is these contrasts that make the islands so appealing and it's easy to see why they're Spain's most popular holiday destination.

Each island is steeped in history, with a strong sense of individual identity. There's a fascinating local culture and the islanders happily welcome any new visitors. Whether your preference is for exploring and hiking, sightseeing or simply soaking up the glorious, hot sun, the choice is simply endless.

TOP ATTRACTIONS

*** Tenerife:** Mount Teide National Park.
*** Lanzarote:** 'lunar' landscape of Timanfaya Park.
** Fuerteventura:** sandy beaches of Jandia peninsula.
** La Palma:** the world's biggest volcanic crater, Taburiente.
** Las Palmas:** the old Vegueta quarter of the city.
* La Gomera:** Columbus's legacy in San Sebastián.
* El Hierro:** the peaceful isolation of El Golfo bay.

Opposite: *The palm-fringed, golden sands of Playa Blanca, Lanzarote; a sun-lover's paradise.*

> **FACTFILE**
>
> **Largest island**: Tenerife 2046km² (790 sq miles).
> **Smallest island**: El Hierro 277km² (107 sq miles).
> **Highest peak**: Mount Teide on Tenerife is 3718m (12,198ft).
> **Government**: Islands divided into two provinces, governor appointed by Spain.
> **Population**: 1,830,000.
> **Most populated island**: Gran Canaria (±720,000).
> **Least populated island**: El Hierro (±8500).

THE LAND

The Canary Islands consist of seven main islands and six minor ones in the Atlantic Ocean. From east to west, **Lanzarote**, **Fuerteventura**, **Gran Canaria**, **Tenerife**, **La Gomera**, **La Palma** and **El Hierro** are the major islands. The minor ones are Isla de Alegranza, Isla Montana Clara, Isla Graciosa, Isla de los Lobos, Roque del Este and Roque del Oeste. The islands are spun out over roughly 450km (280 miles) of the Atlantic, in an area covering 7500km² (2896 sq miles), just off the north-west coast of Africa. It is less than 96km (60 miles) from Fuerteventura to Morocco on the African mainland, and around 1120km (700 miles) northeast to Spain.

Although a long way south of Europe, the Canaries are still 480km (300 miles) north of the Tropic of Cancer. The average latitude of the Canaries is 28° North, and they lie between 13 and 18° west of the zero Meridian. For historical reasons the Canaries belong to Spain, but geographically they are part of **Macaronesia**, a volcanic island group which also comprises the Azores, Madeira and the Cape Verde Islands, all of which have similar topography and indigenous flora.

Opposite: *At the summit of Mount Teide, Tenerife, the highest mountain in Spain.*
Below: *Caldera de Taburiente, La Palma, is an extinct volcano surrounded by snow-capped peaks and jagged pine trees.*

The Islands

The first Canary Islands, Fuerteventura and Lanzarote, were formed nearly 20 million years ago by giant volcanic eruptions. Gran Canaria was the next to emerge, followed by Tenerife and Gomera (about 12 million years ago) and then La Palma and El Hierro (two to three million years ago).

Although all the islands have a common volcanic origin, each has its own identity and character. Five of the islands are extremely mountainous and green: they are rocky, with deep valleys or *barrancos*, volcanic craters, thick forests and fertile plains. Fuerteventura and Lanzarote are bleak and arid, but also immensely interesting in their own right.

THE LAND

Tenerife is the largest island and covers 2046km² (790 sq miles). It is dominated by **Mount Teide**, which at 3718m (12,198ft) is the highest peak on Spanish territory. Next in size is Fuerteventura, covering 1730km² (668 sq miles). Gran Canaria, often termed a continent in miniature owing to its geographical diversity, covers 1533km² (592 sq miles) and is the most heavily populated, with over 650,000 inhabitants. Lanzarote's land area is 862km² (333 sq miles); that of La Palma 730km² (282 sq miles). Both La Gomera, which covers 372km² (144 sq miles) and El Hierro, the most westerly and the smallest island, with an area of 277km² (107 sq miles), are relatively unspoilt. The combined population of the Canary Islands is just under 1,500,000.

Seas and Shores

The deep **Atlantic Ocean** surrounding the islands abounds in fish such as cod, mackerel, sea bass, turbot and sardines. Sportsmen fish for bigeye, bluefin and longtail tuna, marlin, swordfish and various types of shark. All types of shellfish, from lobster and prawns to oysters, litter the shallow pools around the islands' shores.

Climate

Canarios claim that their climate resembles springtime the whole year round. In fact, the southern sides of most islands can seem like a hot summer for most of the year, with cloudless skies and average **temperatures** of 25°C (78°F). The islands boast over 2500 hours of **sunshine** a year

VOLCANOES

The movement of the earth's crust, particularly the clash of continental plates, creates fissures in the thin surface of the globe, which allows molten magma to escape at high pressure. In some cases, the escaping lava may be forced up through a single volcanic cone, such as on Tenerife. This is how Mount Teide was created. Volcanoes can erupt at any time: the last volcanic eruption in the Canaries occurred on La Palma in 1971, when Teneguia exploded. A new landscape was created on Lanzarote from 1730, when a six-year period of volcanic eruptions began, leaving the molten magma just centimetres below the surface.

CANARY ISLANDS	J	F	M	A	M	J	J	A	S	O	N	D
AVERAGE TEMP. °C	18	18	18	19	20	22	24	24	24	25	21	19
AVERAGE TEMP. °F	64	64	64	66	68	72	75	75	75	77	70	66
% HUMIDITY	67	67	66	64	63	62	59	60	65	68	69	67
HOURS OF SUN DAILY	6	8	7	7	8	10	10	8	6	6	5	5
DAYS OF RAINFALL	18	7.5	6	4.9	4	2	1	1	1	2	6	10
RAINFALL mm	36	8	2	11	2	0	0	0	6	3	58	9
RAINFALL in	1.5	0	0	0	0	0	0	0	0	0	2	0

EUPHORBIAS AND MORE

Similar to the Dragon Tree, the curious Euphorbia plant grows mainly in old lava flows and dates back to prehistoric times. Rather like a fleshy plantain, it contains a poisonous sap. Legend has it that the native Guanches poured small quantities of this sap into water in order to stupefy fish, and therefore making them more easy to catch. There are two types of this spurge-like plant on Lanzarote, the pale green *Euphorbia balsamifera*, and *Euphorbia obtusifolia*, called *tabaiba*, plus *Euphorbia canariensis*, a tall, cultivated, cactus-like plant, known locally as *cardon*.

Below: *The Euphorbia plant, indigenous to the islands, grows mainly in old lava flows and contains a poisonous sap.*

and during summer midday temperatures can reach a high of more than 32°C (89°F). When there is **rain** it falls between October and May. It can be **windy** in the summer when the *alisio* blows in from the northwest, and during the autumn the dust brought in by the *sirocco* directly from the Sahara Desert often forms a haze over the islands. **Snow** often lingers on the peak of Mount Teide until May.

Plant Life

You only have to wander through one of the islands' botanical gardens to appreciate the fabulous diversity of flora which abounds in the Canaries. The special climate and generally fertile soil provides ideal conditions. Most striking of the native species is the strange, primeval **dragon tree**, with its dagger-like leaves, which lives for many hundreds of years. Other native plants to look out for include the Canary date palm, Canary pine, gorse, tree ferns and laurelwood.

Spanish settlers brought their favourite plants, vegetables and fruit to the Canaries and, more importantly, **sugar cane** from the Far East. First introduced in the early 1400s, sugar cane became the islands' leading crop and remains a significant export to this day.

From the 15th century onwards the Canaries have been a stopping-off point for ships from around the world, whose crews have introduced numerous tropical

fruits and flowers to
the islands. The prettiest
imported plants include
oleander, bougainvillea,
strelitzia (bird-of-paradise)
and hibiscus. Today the
food index of the islands
reads like a botanist's tour
of the world. Bananas,
oranges, potatoes, tomatoes
and flowers are important
export crops, and the islands'
grapes provide the world
with the celebrated malmsey
wine. On the drier islands,
cacti and succulents such as
prickly pear are widespread.

Above: *Keel-billed toucan, one of the exotic exhibits at Palmitos Parque, Gran Canaria.*

Wildlife

Many species of migratory birds use these isolated landfalls on their Atlantic wanderings. Apart from the common varieties of birdlife, there are curlew, egrets, hoopoe, sandpipers, oyster catchers, and the great grey shrike, or 'butcher bird'. There are many rare birds endemic to the islands, such as the **Fuerteventuran houbara**, the **chat**, the **Canarian buzzard**, the **blue chaffinch** and the common *Serinus canarius* – the **canary**, which was named after the islands. Altogether there are 70 resident species of birds on the islands, with around 200 visitors.

There are no large mammals, poisonous snakes or scorpions on the islands. The **Hierro giant lizard**, the **Canarian oyster catcher** and the **laurel pigeon** are all endangered species indigenous to the Canary Islands.

Some sheep and goats can be seen wandering on pasture land, plateaux, scrubland, and on valley floors, but there are few large herds of domesticated beasts. The local dog, known as a **verdino** because of its greenish tinge, is commonplace, and donkeys are often used as beasts of burden.

SHIPS OF THE DESERT

One of the surprising sights on the Canary Islands is the camel. Not indigenous to the islands, dromedaries (one hump instead of two) were probably brought to Lanzarote from Africa in the 15th century. They are used as beasts of burden and for transport. The camel's diet of thorn scrub and other plants of the *malpais* (badlands) is amply provided on Lanzarote; camels generally have a life expectancy of about 25 years.

ANCIENT CANARIANS

Gofio bread, ritualistic wrestling, the whistling language of Gomera and a wealth of monuments and artefacts testify to ancient Canarians' skills. People lived in caves or small, stone settlements and practised mummification and religious rites. They made stone weapons, ceramics, and farmed pigs and goats in the wide valleys. There are numerous examples of their burial rites, tombs, mausoleums and many mummified bodies.

Below: *Statue of an idealized Guanche chieftain; relics of this Stone Age race can be found throughout the islands.*

HISTORY IN BRIEF

The earliest inhabitants of the Canary Islands belonged to two racial types. Remains of **Cro-Magnon Man** (characterized by broad faces and high foreheads), dating from 3000BC, have been found on the islands. From around the same time a tall, blond-haired, fair-skinned race called **Guanches** also inhabited most of the islands.

Strictly speaking, the word *Guanche* means 'son of Tenerife' in the original island language – the Bimbache tribe lived on El Hierro and the Benahorita on La Palma – but the term is now used generically to describe ethnic Canarians who occupied the islands before the Spanish conquest. No-one has discovered when, or how, they came to the islands but, due to their lack of knowledge regarding boat-building and metals, it must have been at least 2000BC, before the Bronze Age.

Ancient Canarian society was **Stone Age** but not entirely primitive: they had a relatively sophisticated social structure. This varied from island to island, but most were divided into chiefdoms, ruled by a chief who was in turn advised by a council of elders.

Early visitors to the islands included **Phoenicians**, **Carthaginians** and the **Romans** but, as far as we know, no trading links or cultural contacts were established with the locals.

Spanish Conquest

Little seems to be known about the islands until the Genoese explorer Lanzarotto Malocello arrived in 1312 and gave his name to Lanzarote. Both Portugal and Spain sent ships to investigate the Canaries, and in 1344 Pope Clement VI installed the Spaniard Luis de la Cerda as King of the Isles. From then on, a succession of so-called 'kings' were appointed who ruled mostly *in absentia*, having little impact on the islands, whose native inhabitants were probably unaware they were being governed by anyone else. But in 1401 the Canaries were incorporated into the Castilian (Spanish) crown and then the

European conquest of the islands began with a vengeance. In 1402 a Norman, Baron Jean de Béthancourt, and a Spanish nobleman, Gadafir de la Salle, took Lanzarote for the King of Castile. By 1406 they had captured Fuerteventura and La Gomera, but failed to gain more territory in the face of fierce native resistance on the other islands.

For around a century, the native tribes held off the Spanish, who were also dogged by territorial disputes with the Portuguese. In 1477, however, Portugal ceded part of the Canary Islands to Spain and phase two of the Spanish conquest leapt into action. Spanish conquistadores befriended some chiefs and annihilated others. By 1483 Gran Canaria had been conquered and **Pedro de Vera** was appointed as the first Spanish governor of the Canaries. The other islands were captured in swift succession. Tenerife, the last island to fall, was conquered by **Alonso Fernández de Lugo** in 1494 after ferocious fighting. Of the ethnic population, thousands were enslaved, while many intermarried with Spanish settlers or fell victim to European diseases. By the end of the 16th century the ancient Canarians were all but extinct.

> **WHAT'S IN A NAME**
>
> The designation '**Isla Canaria**' appeared for the first time on a Spanish map in 1339, but no-one knows for certain how the islands got their name. In Ancient Greece they were termed the '**Fortunate Isles**'. Pliny the Elder (AD23–79) described an expedition, made about 50 years before his time, from the Roman colony of Mauretania, relating the name Canaris to the island we now know as Gran Canaria. Whether this name originates from the Latin for dog (*canis*), since there certainly were dogs on the island, or whether it comes from the name *canora* for singing bird (which might have been on the island) is anybody's guess!

HISTORICAL CALENDAR

3000BC–AD1500 Islands inhabited by Stone Age people; origins unknown.
1100BC Phoenicians and Carthaginians visit the islands.
1st century AD Expedition from Roman colony of Mauretania to the islands.
1312 Genoese explorer Lanzarotto Malocello names Lanzarote.
1340 Portugal and Spain send ships to investigate islands.
1344 Pope Clement VI appoints Spaniard, Luis de la Cerda, King of the Isles.
1401 Canary Islands are incorporated into the Spanish Crown.
1402–1406 Gadafir de la Salle and Jean de Béthancourt occupy Lanzarote, Fuerteventura and El Hierro.
1478 Captain Rejón founds Las Palmas, Gran Canaria.
1483 Pedro de Vera appointed as first Governor of the Canary Islands.
1492 Columbus visits Canaries. Volcanic eruption on Tenerife.
1494 Tenerife is the last island to fall to Spain.
16th–17th centuries: Spanish settlers establish thriving economy using slave labour
1657 Admiral Blake attacks Spanish treasure fleet.
1731 6 years of volcanic eruptions begin on Lanzarote.
1797 Nelson attacks port of Santa Cruz de Tenerife.
1852 Isabella II declares Canaries a Trade Free Zone.
c1900 Bananas replace sugar cane as mainstay of the islands' economy.
1927 Canary Islands divided into two provinces.
1936 General Franco plots military coup on Tenerife.
1971 Volcanic eruption on La Palma (the most recent).
1982 Regional constitution granted by Spain to the Canary Islands.
1986 The Canary Islands achieve special status within the European Economic Community.

CHRISTOPHORO COLOMBO

Above: *The 15th-century explorer Christopher Columbus, who embarked from the Canary Islands on his epic 1492 voyage of discovery to the New World.*

CHRISTOPHER COLUMBUS

While the last desperate battles for control of the Canary Islands were being fought, Christopher Columbus stopped at the islands to refit his ships while on his voyage of discovery in search of a new sea route to the Indies in 1492. Columbus returned to the islands on subsequent trips. There are several monuments to Columbus on the islands and the elaborate **Casa de Colón** in Las Palmas has many contemporary exhibits.

Spanish Colonialism 1500–1800

The 16th century saw a vast influx of Spanish colonists who used Guanche slave labour in order to establish a profitable economy. The islands rapidly gained economic importance through the cultivation of sugar cane, introduced from Asia, which soon became the island's main source of revenue. Later, wine was to become an economic mainstay. Following Columbus's discovery of the New World in 1492, the islands became a vital staging post for ships, settlers and slaves on their way to and from the Americas.

From the time the Spanish first put their stamp on the islands, however, they became a target for not only the competing navies of **Britain** and **Portugal** but also for a cross-section of marauding pirates. For several hundred years the islanders were besieged by sea-borne attackers: the notorious **Barbary** pirates and **corsairs** conducted hit-and-run raids on the islands. During the 17th and 18th centuries the British, Dutch and Portuguese made many attempts to take the Canaries but were beaten off.

Even the land itself seemed to resent the colonists. During the 1700s, volcanoes erupted with frightening regularity. In 1731, seismic disturbance began on Lanzarote and lasted six years, transforming the land into an eerie moonscape. However, undeterred by harassment from the sea and the ravages of nature, the islanders took to political in-fighting to prove their dominance over one another.

Factionalism and Free Trade 1800–1900

Both **Gran Canaria** and **Tenerife** squabbled over which was to become the dominant island. The Canaries also took on the might of the mother country, Spain, in order to establish their identity. Even now the islanders deny that they are Europeans, stating that they are African. Certainly the islands are much nearer the African mainland than they are to Madrid.

HISTORY IN BRIEF

The in-fighting resulted in the eventual establishment of a Permanent Island Council, or *cabildo*, of Gran Canaria in Las Palmas in 1808. From this time, the *cabildo* system became adopted throughout the islands, each appointed from mainland Spain and responsible for administering their own separate affairs. Las Palmas became the capital of Gran Canaria in 1820, but Santa Cruz de Tenerife was established as the capital of the whole archipelago in 1822. The Canaries were declared a **free-trade zone** (duty-free) in 1852 by Isabella II in order to stimulate the economy. The development of the harbour of Las Palmas was begun in 1882 and by the end of the century, bananas had replaced sugar as the islands' main crop.

From the middle of the 19th century, a new invasion had begun, that of **tourism**. It coincided with the advent of the steamship and when the routes to and around South Africa were established. Visitors arrived in the Canaries by boat from Western Europe, beginning an influx of tourists which was only halted during the two World Wars. There were, however, several hiccups in the political stability of the islands which interrupted the tourist trade, particularly towards the end of the 19th century, when the examples of **Filipino** and **Cuban** insurrection against Spanish rule stirred Canario patriotism.

NELSON'S ARM

Lord Horatio Nelson was a 38-year-old admiral when he led a landing party of English marines in 1797, attacking Santa Cruz de Tenerife. Grapeshot raked his gallant band, and the heavy fire drove the British back to their ship, the *Theseus*, which was moored out in the bay.

A total of 226 British sailors were killed in the fray, and another 123 wounded. When the survivors carried Nelson on board they noticed that his right arm was badly damaged. It had to be amputated. The tattered flags that Nelson's contingent carried into battle now hang in the parish church of Santa Cruz and in the Paso Alto castle is the cannon, the *Tiger*, that fired the telling shot at Nelson's arm.

Left: *Banana plantation, Tenerife. By the end of the 19th century, bananas had become the islands' most important cash crop.*

Above: *Over the years, the Canary Islands have built up a chain of luxurious accommodation, including this parador in Teide National Park, Tenerife.*

A Tenuous Neutrality

Both Spain and the Canary Islands remained neutral during the two world wars. While maritime traffic dropped off during both periods, there are rumours that **General Franco** had secret dealings with the Germans during **World War II**, giving almost the entire Jandia peninsula to a German engineer. Stories abound of night landings of German submarines and underground bunkers. It was from these positions that the Nazis were supposed to have preyed on Allied shipping.

The 20th Century

Before the outbreak of World War I the Canary Islands were still strategically important as a stopping-off point in the Atlantic seaways, but war seriously interrupted the islands' trade. This was followed by an exodus of islanders to the New World.

The islands were divided into two provinces in 1927: the **Western Islands**, governed from Tenerife, and those ruled from Gran Canaria, the **Eastern Islands**. In 1936, **General Francisco Franco**, military governor of the Canaries, planned a military coup in Spain while on Tenerife, which eventually led to the formation of a Spanish Republic. During the **Spanish Civil War**, and continuing through Franco's dictatorship (1936–1975), the Canary Islands were largely neglected by Spain and by the world's tourists. The importance of the Canaries as a stepping-stone to the New World and the Far East declined with the advent of aircraft and the opening up of the **Suez Canal**. Tourism, however, took off again during the 1960s, quickly becoming the islands' main source of convertible revenue, as incoming visitors increased from a few thousand to the several million who are now welcomed each year.

GOVERNMENT AND ECONOMY
System of Government
The Canaries are part of Spain, a country that hashad a constitutional monarchy since 1978. The islands consist of two provinces which since 1982 have been one autonomous region (there are 17 altogether in Spain), responsible for self-government. Spain is part of the European Union.

The seven main islands in the archipelago have comprised two of Spain's 50 provinces since 1927. **Las Palmas Province** is made up of Gran Canaria, Fuerteventura and Lanzarote; **Santa Cruz de Tenerife Province** comprises Tenerife, La Palma, La Gomera and El Hierro. Both provinces have civil and military governors appointed from Madrid. The **Gobinero de Canarias** (Government of the Canaries) is responsible for all domestic Canarian matters such as health services, roads and water supply. Each island is divided into smaller administrative units (*municipios*). There has always been friction between the seven Canary Islands governing bodies, especially between Tenerife, now the capital of the Western Islands, and Gran Canaria, the capital of the Eastern Islands.

The **Union of the Canarian People** and the more radical **Movement for Self-Determination and Independence** are both pressurizing for total independence from Spain. This is not supported by the majority of the people. Instead, many Canarians feel Spain should economically support their islands, as they put the blame for their poverty on Spain's neglect of the Canaries during General Franco's dictatorship.

Above: *The Canary Islands' flag, adopted in 1982 when the islands became an autonomous region. The colours were taken from the naval flags of Santa Cruz de Tenerife and Las Palmas.*
Below: *Volcanic soils on Lanzarote are fertile; here, workers gather the onion harvest at La Haria.*

> **PARADORES**
>
> With more than 150 years of tourism, the Canary Islands have built up an infrastructure of holiday accommodation, from high rise hotels on beach resorts to guest houses located on the smaller islands. The Spanish, however, have a passion for converting some of their fabulous castles and palaces into superior accommodation known as *paradores*. This trend has spread to the Canaries, which now boast five paradores and one *hosteleria*.

Economic Development

The economy of the islands rode a stormy sea for many hundreds of years. The ravages of nature, particularly the many volcanic eruptions, famine and regular attacks by pirates, dogged the Canaries' early prosperity. The fertile black soil and an equable climate, however, made for an ideal agricultural environment. At one time, the islands' economy was almost entirely based on sugar, wine, tomatoes, bananas and cochineal.

Today, bananas, tobacco, coffee, potatoes, tomatoes, avocados, dates and citrus fruits, vines and carpets of flowers thrive in the near perfect climate. However, because the subsidies to banana-growers in Central America and the Caribbean have lowered the price of the fruit, many banana farmers are turning their attention more to lucrative crops such as exotic vegetables, flowers, pot plants and pineapples

Industry

With their proximity to the European mainland and the plethora of cheap charter flights, the Canary Islands represent one of the most convenient destinations for travellers seeking year-round sun, sand and sea.

Tourism is now shaping the islands' future: indeed, some islands depend on its revenue. There are airports on six of the seven major islands and one is under construction on La Gomera. New roads have opened up the wealth of scenery which abounds throughout the Canaries. Today the islands are a mecca for tourists from Germany, Scandinavia, Britain, and mainland Spain. Of the 43 million tourists who visit Spain annually, the Canaries attract almost a quarter of that number alone.

Below: *The black sandy beach of Playa de la Arena, Tenerife, a year-round holiday destination.*

THE PEOPLE

Today's Canarios are a proud, friendly and easy-going people, willing to help and delighted to show visitors their culture and countryside. They are fiercely *Canarios* rather than *Peninsulares*, which is what they call the Spanish. Having been a bridge between Europe and the rest of the world for so long, there is a great ethnic mix of people who are fully integrated into society. Each islander has his own identity within the Canary Islands. Those from Gran Canaria are known as **Canarios**; the people on Fuerteventura are called **Fuerteventurans** and those on Lanzarote, **Lanzarotenos**. On Tenerife the people are **Tinerfeños**; on Palma, **Palmeros**; on La Gomera, **Gomeros**; and on El Hierro, **Herreños**. Evidence of intermarriage between early colonists and **Guanches** is still evident in the features of many islanders today.

Illiteracy is still a problem on the islands: at the end of Franco's dictatorship it was estimated to be as high as 50% in some rural areas and stands at between 7–10% today, far higher than on mainland Spain. Society is also changing rapidly due to worker migration from the villages to the resorts.

Language

The universal language in Spain is **Castilian Spanish** (textbook Spanish), but the dialect used on the Canary Islands is more like that of Latin America. The last 's' in a word is often not pronounced. A 'z' is not pronounced *th* as in Spain, but as an *s*. A 'c' before 'i' or 'e' is pronounced *s*. Words are often curtailed, and are sometimes run together in a sentence, making the individual words difficult to understand.

Many **Guanche** words have remained, particularly in place names. These often begin with the letters 'gua', which is pronounced *wah*. Coincidentally, this prefix

Above: *Tinerfeños in traditional dress: bright colours and geometric designs are a Guanche legacy.*

THE CANARIO

The typical Canario male is a caricature unto himself. In the Canarian writer, Pancho Guerra's stories, his name was Pepe Monagas, his wife Camildita. The island's sugar, rum and food gave him a large stomach, around which he would traditionally wear a wide sash and where a special local knife would protrude. A loose shirt would be covered by an open waistcoat, and, on his head, the archetypal Canarian would wear a battered old hat. Below baggy trousers, he would wear a pair of ill-fitting boots. Today, the only remnant of the Pepe figure is in the language and the macho moustache with the cigar stub. On festive occasions the Canarios wear distinctive costumes, varying from island to island.

occurs frequently in the Cuban language and can be traced back to the pre-Columbian days of the **Taino Amerindians**. A typical Cuban import is the name for the local buses – 'gua-gua', pronounced *wah-wah*.

Local patois or dialects are heard on some islands and in the countryside. It is perhaps better for the visitor to avoid trying to learn the local dialect and to stick to mainland Spanish, although English, and most western European languages, are widely understood. Outside the main towns and resort areas, it's a good idea to carry a small dictionary or phrase book.

Religion

Although pagan for many thousands of years under the ancient Guanche civilization, the conquering Spaniards brought **Roman Catholicism** with them to the islands. It is now the dominant religion. There are numerous churches dotted throughout the islands. However, there are Anglican and other denomination churches, a couple of synagogues and a mosque. Times of services are usually announced in Spanish and English outside most churches and visitors should observe these times when visiting the islands' historic churches.

EL SILBO

The unique whistling language of La Gomera, *el silbo*, is legendary, invented for communications over long distances of difficult terrain, most probably by the native Guanche population. Apparently the *silbadores* can be understood up to 8km (5 miles) away. It is still in use today and fishermen and farmers find it very handy for keeping in touch with each other while out of sight at sea, or on the steep-sided fields. A good place to hear the silbo is in the grounds of Gomera's only parador, where gardeners use it to communicate with each other.

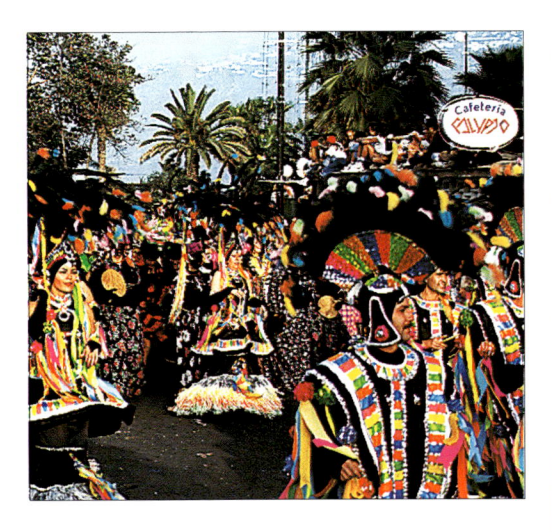

Left: *Carnival-goers often dress according to themes; their magnificent costumes can take up to a year to make.*
Opposite: *Carnaval: a 10-day springtime street party where locals and tourists dance to exuberant Latin beats.*

Canary Island Festivals

Fiestas (festivals) are the traditional method for celebrating saints' days and religious occasions. Most fiestas are of a religious nature, and each island has its own patron saint. **Candelaria** is the patron saint of the Canary Islands as a whole and the patron saint of Spain is **Santiago**, or St James. Don't miss the festival of **Corpus Christi**, when islanders spend painstaking hours making carpets of sand and flowers, or **Carnaval** (Carnival), which rivals that of Rio de Janeiro. September's **Santisímo Cristo** fiesta is spectacular, with fireworks and folk dancing, and Las Palmas' pilgrimage of **Nuestra Señora de la Luz** includes a procession of boats. There are numerous festivals throughout the islands, each one an enchanting mix of local culture, spectacle and tremendous fun.

Fiestas can also take the form of pilgrimages (*romerías*) and agricultural parades, accompanied by satirical songs (*murgas*). Many of these celebrations are visual feasts, with participants dressed in fabulous costumes and plazas decorated in bunting. Some of the most stunning decorations are the floral carpets which you can see at **La Orotava** and **La Laguna** on Tenerife,

---

HISTORIC CATHEDRALS AND CHURCHES

Even though the islands are divided into two provinces, the Canary Islands have only one cathedral: **Santa Ana** (dating from 1497) in Las Palmas (Gran Canaria). The locals, however, also call the impressive neo-Gothic parish church of Arucas, also on Gran Canaria, a cathedral.

Many of the islands' major churches, such as the **Church of Nuestra Señora de la Asunción** on La Gomera, date from the late 15th century. Also important are **Nuestra Señora del Pino** (1515) in Teror, Gran Canaria; the ruined **Iglesia Santa María de Betancuria**, Fuerteventura (1539); and the 16th-century **Iglesia Nuestra Señora de la Concepción**, Santa Cruz de Tenerife.

The 15th-century **Church of Nuestra Señora de Guadeloupe** in Teguise (Lanzarote) is thought to be the oldest church in the entire group of islands.

CARNAVAL

With pagan derivations steeped in the mists of time, Carnaval, as we know it now, is not a Christian invention. The word comes from the Latin *carne vale* – *carne* meaning meat, and *vale* meaning farewell – hence farewell to meat.

The celebration recognizes the final days of feasting before Ash Wednesday. Gran Canaria celebrates during the last two weeks of February, but throughout the islands, celebrations can last until late March. Processions and bands, masqueraders and itinerant musicians parade the streets accompanied by decorated floats and street vendors.

and the sand, grass, pebble and flower patterns around the cathedral in **Las Palmas**. Each island, city, town and village seems to have its own patron saint. Certainly the Canarian joke of a fiesta happening somewhere in the islands every day seems to ring true!

Firework displays, horse parades, bonfires, parades of religious statues and icons, traditional folk dancing and ritual enactments are all part of the fiesta fun. In addition, fiestas often mingle pagan customs and religious elements – a reminder of the long-standing dependency of the islanders on nature. A number of these celebrations date back to the dark, mysterious times of the Guanches. These include the **Rain Fiesta** of Telde and the **Rama Fiesta** of Agaete on Gran Canaria. Often local historical events are incorporated in the religious festivities, like the re-enactment of the repulsing of **Sir Francis Drake** from Fuerteventura and Gran Canaria, or the two-century-old ritual of beating off swarms of locusts which once threatened crops in Guia, Gran Canaria.

Carnivals give the islanders yet another opportunity to let their hair down. These generally do not have any religious significance, being mainly a social event for the local community to enjoy the parades, stalls and folk dancing. *Ferias* (town fairs) are also a popular diversion, often held in conjunction with the local carnival.

Right: *Revellers make final adjustments to their appearance before the Mardi Gras parade, Tenerife.*
Opposite: *Religious procession in Santa Cruz de la Palma passing by the replica of Columbus's ship, the* Santa María.

Sport and Recreation

There are some unique Canarian sports and pastimes which date back thousands of years, at least to the days of the Guanche civilization, if not further. **Canarian wrestling**, or *lucha canaria*, which was developed by the ancients, is famous throughout the world and its rules are strict and rigid. Teams generally consist of two league teams of 12 *luchadores* (participants). Two barefoot contestants stand inside a 10m (33ft), sand-covered circle, in a stadium called a *terrero*, and attempt to throw each other to the ground. Individual bouts are known as *bregas*. Judging is complicated and requires much debate before a decision is declared by the judge. Canarian

MAJOR FESTIVALS

5 January Procession of the Magi: Santa Cruz de Tenerife and Las Palmas de Gran Canaria.
January–February Canary Islands Music Festival: Las Palmas de Gran Canaria and La Orotava, Tenerife.
February–March Gran Carnaval: Las Palmas de Gran Canaria, Santa Cruz de Tenerife and Puerto de la Cruz. Winter Festivals (Sixth week before Palm Sunday) Las Palmas de Gran Canaria.
March–April Holy Week: Las Palmas de Gran Canaria, Santa Cruz de Tenerife and La Laguna Tenerife. Opera Festival: Las Palmas de Gran Canaria and Santa Cruz de Tenerife.
29 April Royal incorporation of Gran Canaria into Castilian Crown: Las Palmas.
April–May Spanish Festivals of theatre, ballet, music etc: Las Palmas de Gran Canaria and Santa Cruz de Tenerife.
May Spring Festivals and Opera: Santa Cruz de Tenerife.
1–5 May Founding of Santa Cruz de Tenerife.

20 May San Isidro Labrador Festival: Los Realejos, Tenerife.
30 May Canary Islands regional holiday. Corpus Christi Floral carpet festival: Las Palmas de Gran Canaria, La Laguna, Tenerife, and Villa de Mazo, La Palma. Octava de Corpus La Orotava, Tenerife.
21–30 June (every five years) Nuestra Señora de las Nieves Festival: Santa Cruz de la Palma.
21–30 June (every four years) Nuestra Señora de las Nieves Festival: Valverde, El Hierro.
First Sunday of July San Benito Abad Festival: La Laguna Tenerife
14 July San Buenaventura Festival: Betancuria, Fuerteventura.
16 July La Virgen del Carmen Festival: Santa Cruz de Tenerife.
25 July Santiago de Apostol, Gáldar and San Bartolomé Festival and Defence against Nelson's attack: Gran Canaria and Santa Cruz de Tenerife.
5 August Virgen de las Nieves Festival: Santa Cruz de la Palma and Agaete, Gran Canaria.

16 August San Roque Festival: Garachico, Tenerife.
25 August San Gines Festival: Arrecife, Lanzarote.
28 August San Agustin Festival: Arafo, Tenerife.
6–8 September La Virgen de Pinto Festival: Teror, Gran Canaria.
7–15 September El Santisimo Cristo Festival: La Laguna, Tenerife.
11 September El Charco Celebrations: Aldea de San Nicolas, Gran Canaria.
Sunday after 17 September El Cristo del Calvario Festival: Icod de los Viños, Tenerife.
12 October Celebration of Columbus's discovery of America in 1492.
Second Saturday in October Nuestra Señora de la Luz Festival – (best procession): Las Palmas de Gran Canaria.
November–December Opera Festival: Santa Cruz de Tenerife.
13 December Santa Lucia Festival: Gran Canaria.
26 December Canary Islands regional holiday.

Above: *Windsurfing, one of the many watersports to be enjoyed in the Canaries.*

WORLD RECORDS

Huge shoals of fish run the gauntlet of Canarian fishing boats especially between the islands of Fuerteventura and Lanzarote and mainland Africa. The attraction for visitors is the opportunity to try their hand at deep-sea fishing. No licence is required for this increasingly popular sport. Many world record fish have been caught off the islands' coasts. Swordfish, white marlin, blue marlin, bluefin, yellowfin and a tuna known locally as *atún de ojo grand*, are popular for weight records.

---

wrestling is practised throughout the islands and is a popular tourist attraction, as well as a feature of most fiestas. To commemorate the history of Canarian wrestling, many matches are held at original Guanche strongholds. Historians have noted that Canarian wrestling is similar to that practised by the ancient Egyptians.

The other unique national sport is called *juego de palo*, or *banot*, the stick game. This is also said to date from Guanche times. It is rather like fencing but instead of using swords, contestants use long poles.

On Tenerife and La Palma, islanders specialize in a method of getting around in a land of deep ravines and rugged gorges. They employ a technique of pole-vaulting known locally as the *salto del regaton de la garrocha*, or **pike leap**. Here amazing feats are performed with the use of a pole of around 2.5m (6½ft) in length. The contestants leap down the mountain sides with a skill derived from the ancient inhabitants of the island.

Canarios have a passionate love of cock-fighting and dog-fighting, which are not illegal on the islands. However, bullfighting has never been popular, unlike on the Spanish mainland.

The sea offers the tourist a great variety of wonderful sporting opportunities. A unique watersport is the *vela latina*, a yachting race involving short 'Optimist' boats with vast triangular sails. Races and regattas are held at most weekends wherever conditions are right.

Yachting, **sailing**, **power-boat racing**, **water-skiing** and **windsurfing** are popular pastimes throughout the islands. Because the sea temperature ranges from around 22°C (72°F) to 19°C (66°F), and the sea abounds in many interesting volcanic and coral formations, teeming with marine life, **scuba diving** and **snorkelling** are also extremely popular. Visibility in some waters can be up to 40m (130ft) and there are also several fascinating underwater national parks around the islands for the preservation of undersea life. The **Gulf Stream** which sweeps past the islands also brings in prize-winning fish, making **deep-sea fishing** a main attraction for devotees. Freshwater reservoir fishing is also possible on some islands, but a licence must be obtained first from the Ministry of Agriculture and Fisheries.

Other activity sports, apart from **hiking**, **rambling**, **walking** and **climbing**, include **mountain-biking**, **hunting**, **riding**, **tennis**, **squash**, **golf** and **soccer**, a favourite with Canarios. There are numerous dog tracks, horse-racing and show-jumping clubs and motor-rallying contests. The **El Corte Inglés** motor rally on Gran Canaria is internationally famous.

Food and Drink

Owing to the great influx of tourists to the Canaries, foreign cuisine abounds throughout the islands. There are restaurants, however, which not only serve traditional Canarian food, but also local dishes of the particular islands. Restaurants are graded with a 'fork' symbol: five forks being the best. Meals are generally light, being more digestible in a warm climate.

A variety of fresh vegetables, fruit and fish forms the basis of Canarian cuisine. The traditional island food is *gofio*, a kind of flour meal made from toasted cereals. *Gofio* is used to make the island's celebrated nougat and is often a substitute for bread. Another staple food is *papas arugadas*, small potatoes cooked in their skins with a lot of salt.

WALKING TOURS

One of the best ways to enjoy the climate and countryside of the Canary Islands is by taking a walking tour. Leaving the tourist resorts behind, a wealth of experiences and sights await the more adventurous traveller. It is best to follow one of the suggested walks rigidly, as waymarking has not yet reached much of the Canarian landscape. Maps are essential, and a weather-eye is important, as conditions can change rapidly. A genuine respect for the countryside and its people is also an important ingredient for a successful expedition. Good boots, sun and rain protection, sufficient water and a good head for heights are also invaluable on some of the more ambitious walks.

Below: *A mouth-watering variety of local dishes on offer at a food stall in Puerto de la Cruz, Tenerife.*

Above: *Locally caught fish drying in the sun on Lanzarote's northern coast.*
Above right: *Vegetables grow in abundance on the islands. Here, corn is hung out to dry.*

GOFIO

When Spanish colonists met opposition from the local Guanche tribes on Fuerteventura, their attempts at obtaining a forceful submission failed. They then hoped to employ the alternative weapon of starvation.

This also failed, as the local *majoreros* began cultivating an indigenous glasswort plant from which they produced a native meal, *gofio*. In the 16th century, Indian corn, or maize, was introduced as a substitute. This quickly became the island's traditional dish. *Gofio* is still a local island delicacy – made from a mixture of wheat and maize flour.

Dishes imported from Spain include small, tasty dishes of bite-size morsels known as *tapas*, *gazpacho* (cold soup) and *paella* (saffron rice with vegetables, meat and fish). Tenerife is famous for its spicy sauces such as *salsa mojo picon*, made from peppers, garlic and other hot ingredients. La Gomera specializes in *salsa verde*, featuring coriander and parsley, which is particularly good with fish.

Meat eaters will find rabbit (*conejo*), chicken (*pollo*), kid goat, or wild pork, often marinated in a sauce of vinegar, herbs and garlic (*salmorejo*). Stews (*puchero* or *estofado*) are commonplace in the Eastern Province, often eaten with *gofio*. *Potaje canariense* is a vegetable and tomato soup thickened with *gofio*. Other favourite traditional soups include *sancocho* (meat, potatoes and vegetables) and *sopa de berros* (watercress and herb soup). *Sopa de millo* is a thin maize and meat broth made with *gofio*.

Fresh **fish** is naturally always on offer. There's a mouthwatering variety of exotic and everyday fish, which is usually cooked plain – either grilled, boiled or fried. Fish casseroles (*cazuela canaria*) are universally popular. Particular fish to look out for include *la vieja*, *cherne* (stone bass), grouper, *corvina* and horse mackerel on Tenerife, and *tollo* on Lanzarote. Some islands serve *sancocho*, a fish salad with hot sauce.

Desserts usually include the delicious fruit, such as mangoes, paw paw, cherimoya and bananas. Hierro is renowned for its cheesecake (*quesadillas*) and La Palma for its almond cheese. Another delicacy includes *bienmesabe* which contains almond cream, egg and honey. *Tirijalas*, or *torrijas*, are sweet, maize-flour fritters soaked in syrup; *Frangollo* are sweet pancakes made from honey, almonds, raisins, milk and corn. *Platanos fritas* are fried bananas sprinkled with lemon juice, brandy and sugar – delicious.

El Hierro produces some of the most exquisite **cheeses**, made from a mixture of cow, goat and sheep's milk. *Queso Herreño* comes either smoked (*ahumada*), or mature (*curada*).

Drinks include rum, honey-rum (*ron miel*), **malmsey** wine and red wine (*vino tinto* from Tacoronte, Tenerife, is the most widely available). Rum and coke is known as *cubatas*. Coffee is an important produce on the Canaries and *cafe solo* is small, strong, sweet and black. *Cafe con leche* is milky coffee, often made with sweet condensed milk.

The Arts

The islands have been the cradle of many celebrated writers, artists and musicians. **José Eugenio**, the famous 18th-century goldsmith, was a Canario, and Guia, on Gran Canaria was the birthplace of the 18th-century sculptor, **José Lujan Pérez**. Las Palmas was the birthplace of novelist **Benito Pérez Galdós**. **Pancho Guerra,** the writer, was also a Canario. Local artist **Néstor de la Torre** launched a campaign to revive Canarian folk art and architecture, and designed the Canarian Village in Las Palmas. Architect, design guru and enviromentalist, **César Manrique** was Lanzarote's most famous citizen.

> **TAPAS**
>
> *Tapas* are a Spanish speciality and they come in a wonderful variety of tastes. These snacks consist of small pieces of fish, shrimp, octopus (*pulpo*), squid (*calamares*), shellfish, and meat, pork or goat, marinated in sauces (*mojo*), with a variety of small plates of side salads and olives. *Tapas* can also be small slices of *tortilla*, a flan, or omelette, with potatoes, onions and vegetables. *Ropa vieja*, literally 'old woman's clothes', is another popular *tapa*, and is a small bowl of thick stew.

Below: *A characteristically simple mural by the celebrated Canarian artist César Manrique at Tahiche, Lanzarote.*

> **CESAR MANRIQUE**
>
> Born in Lanzarote in 1920, César Manrique is the Canaries most celebrated artist. With a string of exhibitions and shows, Manrique turned his skills to building the powerfully contemporary **Monumento Campesino** in 1968. Other striking artistic additions to the Lanzarote landscape, installed by the artist, are the **Jamenos del Agua**, on the northeast coast, and the **El Diablo** restaurant in Timanfaya National Park. He was killed in a car crash in 1992.

MEDIA

You'll find several foreign-language newspapers aimed at tourists in the Canary Islands: the main ones are *Lanzarote Holiday Gazette* and *Island Connections* (Tenerife). Tourist offices, hotels and many bars have free guides listing what's on and where to go. All the main foreign newspapers are available in the towns.

Below: *The wooden balcony surrounding the second-storey windows of the basilica in Candelaria is a typical architectural feature designed to give extra shade.*

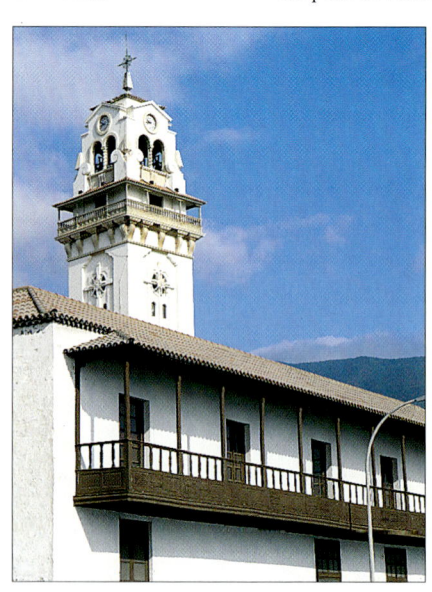

Secindino Delgado, the patriot and founder of the newspaper *El Guanche*, was born in the Canaries, as was the mother of José Marti, Cuba's national hero. **Miguel de Unamuno**, a Spanish poet exiled on the island of Fuerteventura in 1924, enthused over its landscape. Local musical groups such as **Los Majuelos**, the **Sabandenos** and **Taburiente** have quite a following world-wide.

The Canary Islands are home to a wealth of museums and art galleries, apart from the numerous churches which house collections of precious artwork. In Las Palmas the **Santa Ana Cathedral** has a wonderful museum of Aztec and pre-Columbian treasure, and most island capitals have fascinating museums packed with local treasures. On La Palma, a concrete replica of Columbus's ship, the **Santa María**, houses a Maritime Museum, as does the **Casa de Colón** in Las Palmas.

In La Orotava, Tenerife, the **Casa Tafuriaste** has one of the best collections of regional ceramics in all of Spain. In Valle Guerra, on Tenerife, the **Casade Carta Ethnological Museum** has a comprehensive collection of regional costumes, and the **Castillo San José**, in Arrecife, on Lanzarote, is the home of the Museum of Contemporary Art. Probably the best place to see a complete cross-section of Canarian art, crafts and culture is at the **Pueblo Canario Museum**, the model Canary Island village in Doramas Park, Las Palmas.

Architecture

Typical Canarian architecture encompasses a variety of styles. Round, stone dwellings, and almost inaccessible necropoli carved out of rock, stand as testament to the building skills of the ancients.

Modern, or western, architecture was brought by the Spanish to the islands. Spanish building design had been influenced by many hundreds of years of Moorish occupation. The Canary Islands are often bereft of water, co-incidentally an important factor in Spanish or Moorish house design. In early architecture, most houses were built around a central courtyard, or patio, focused on a well. The central well was so important that Moorish architects embellished the well with exotic and expensive tiles. This trend was carried on in the Canary Islands. Often rainwater was collected in butts or large stone jars from the roofs and ornate spouts can still be seen protruding from many roofs.

Given the climate, the Moorish building designs (a style which is known as *mudéjar*), were naturally adopted in the Canaries. Originally without any air-conditioning, it was essential to construct houses with an effective air flow, guaranteed by the ever-present patio, a central feature of Canarian architecture. Styles of architecture range from colonial Baroque, through Rococo, Victorian Gothic, to Art Nouveau and Art Deco, and to the modern and futuristic designs of Lanzarote architect **César Manrique**. They also reflect both the artistic styles of the Old and New World as several churches sport traditional Mexican designs, derived from the Spanish conquest of the Aztecs and Mayans.

Patios were usually filled with shady trees and surrounded on all four sides by a colonnaded cloister. In a typical old Canarian townhouse, protection from the heat of the sun and occasional rainstorms was paramount in colonial building design. Columned, covered walkways extending the length of the house frontage were also popular features, many of which can be seen in the grandiose palaces and early official residences on the plazas of the old squares. Cobbled streets, plazas and alleyways are another feature of colonial architecture, worn smooth over the centuries by boot leather, hooves, and the wheels of countless horse-drawn carriages.

Above: *Traditional Canarian buildings were designed to give protection from the sun.*

THE CANARIAN COURTYARD

Features of the enclosed courtyard are typical of many of the very early Cuban buildings. In order to increase the amount of shade in the cobbled courtyard, trees were often planted in strategic positions. A well often featured in the courtyard.

Later adaptations in courtyard design sometimes included terracotta spouts protruding from the gulleys of the roofs of the balcony, from which rainwater was caught in large vats.

Above: *Many architectural details reflect a Moorish influence.*
Below: *Folk dancing and traditional music are still very popular in the islands.*

PARALLELS WITH CUBA

Just over half a century ago, many islanders emigrated to the Caribbean, taking their skills and culture with them. Sugar, Cuba's main produce, was first planted on the island by Columbus, who brought the plant from the Canaries. Today, factories in the Canaries process much of Cuba's second product, tobacco. Experts are also now comparing the similarities between prehistoric Taino drawings or carvings found on Cuba with the rock paintings of the Guanche of the Canaries. The strategic location of the twin Free Ports of Las Palmas and Tenerife, compares in importance to that of Havana.

Many Canarian houses are dazzling architectural gems, with whitewashed walls and red-tiled roofs, surrounded by a wide patio and cloister-like roofing overhanging the main structure. A balcony usually runs around the inside of the building, overlooking the cobbled patio, and railed around with finely turned hardwood support, often of Cuban mahogany or Canarian laurel.

Typically, governor's palaces and grand villas were also designed to stay cool. Wide doors, opening out on to the patio, provided a through-draught of air, and high windows in the outside wall ensured excellent air-conditioning. The deep, long windows around the second storey, on the outside of the building, were enclosed on three sides by fretwork screens, copying the Moorish style. The windows could be closed from the inside with shutters. Under the second storey, long windows were topped by individual narrow, tiled roofs. These windows stood out from the wall of the house with their wooden fretwork screens and together with their tiled roofing and own screens, light and air flowed freely into the lower-floor rooms.

Music and Dance

This is the favourite Canarian pastime for celebrating. At every opportunity the islanders take great delight in performing their unique variations of both dance and song. The *timple*, only found on the Canary Islands and in Cuba, is a small stringed instrument somewhere

between a guitar and an ukelele. It was created in
Teguise where it is still made. The *timple* forms the
background to two local folk dances: the *isa*, a jolly,
country dance, and the *folia*, a more dignified, dance.
Exhibits of traditional Canarian music and dance, or
verbena, are held regularly throughout the islands.

Crafts

The wide variety of woods which grow on most of the
islands has been the basis for much of Canary craftsmanship. Furniture, cedar chests and weaving looms
are prime examples of the islanders' skills. **Basketwork**
made from *cana* (cane) make ideal souvenirs.

Most of the islands' craftwork is extremely practical,
and can be very decorative. *Vara* (twigwork), made from
strips of chestnut, can be very attractive. *Palanqueta*
work, made from date stems, is also a popular island
craft. Crafts to look out for include the islands' unique
glazed pottery, a legacy of the ancient Canarians,
traperas (rag rugs), silk woven cloths, hand-embroidered
bordados (tablecloths), costumed rag dolls, woollen
shawls and polished green volcanic stone jewellery.
Musical instruments like **castanets** (*chacaras*) and the
local stringed *timple* make interesting gifts.

The most attractive Canarian craft souvenirs are the
beautiful openwork or **embroidery**. The delicacy of the
workmanship which local women put into producing
this cloth is incredible – the most exquisite embroidery
comes from Tenerife and La Palma.

Above: *Olive oil was once stored in clay jars like these, now used as decorative planters.*
Below: *Beautifully hand-embroidered tablecloths make excellent souvenirs.*

A DYING BUG

In 1825, agronomists introduced an industry to the
Canary Islands, based around
a tiny insect, *Dactylopius coc-
cus*, which lives exclusively
on a variety of cacti, from
which cochineal is extracted
by crushing the bugs.
Cochineal, a crimson dye,
earned the islanders a brief
respite from economic
decline, when it became the
Canary Islands' most valuable
export. Today, only a few
farmers produce the dye,
which involves the fastidious
picking of the insects from
prickly cactus leaves.

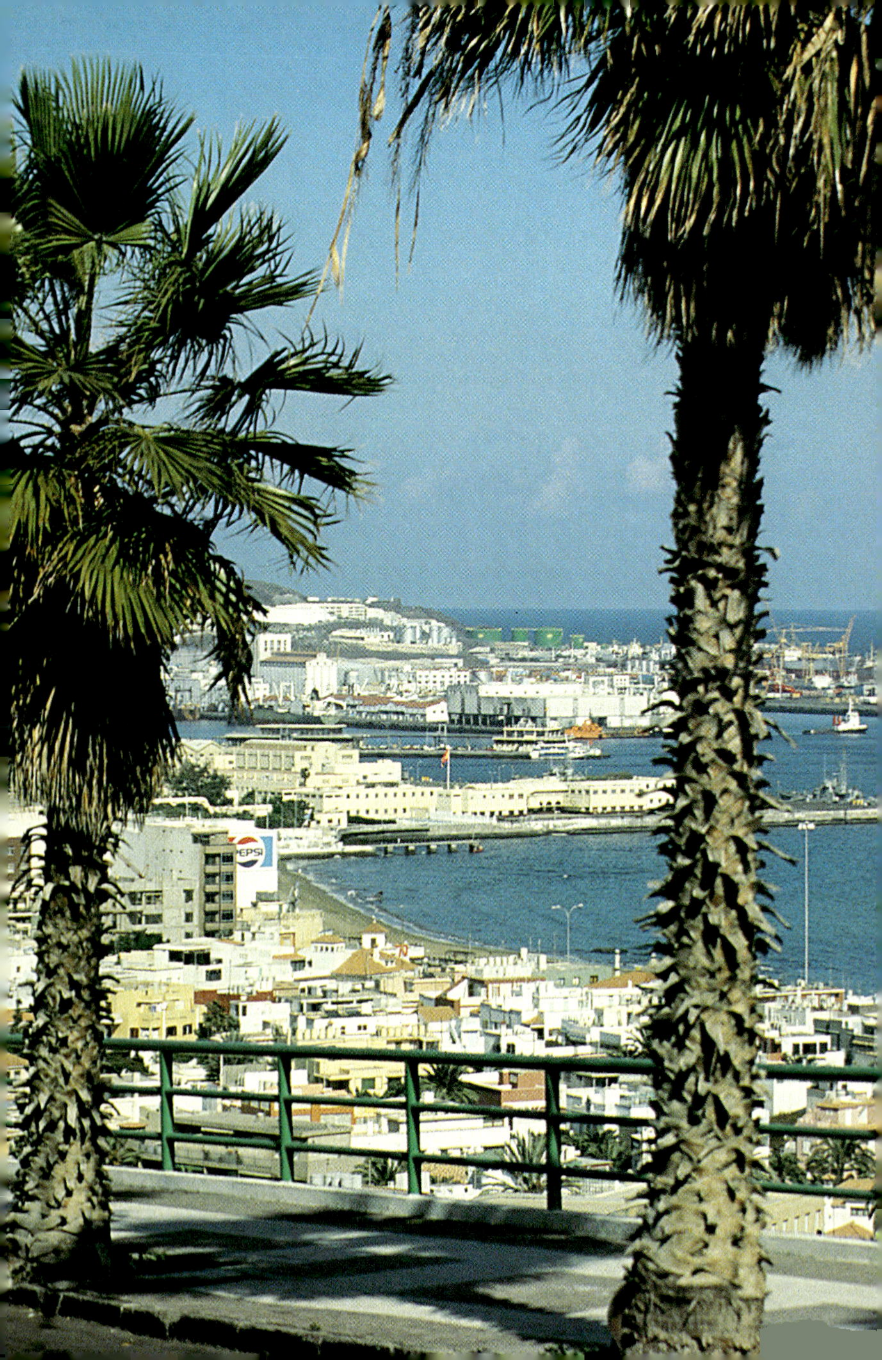
PEPSI

2
Las Palmas

More than just the capital of the eastern Canary Islands, Las Palmas today is a sprawling, cosmopolitan, multi-racial metropolis, similar to many large ports around the world but with a vibrancy and charm all of its own. Its population has doubled during the past 30 years to over 355,000 inhabitants and more than half of the Canarios now live here.

It's easy to see why. There's a wealth of interesting **museums** covering everything from Cro-Magnon man to Columbus, and several delightful churches. One of the top sights is the **Pueblo de Canario** in Doramas Park, an idealized Canarian village that presents a microcosm of the way island life used to be, complete with exuberant folk-dancing displays.

Early visitors included Phoenicians, Carthaginians and Moors, but it wasn't until the Spanish arrived in 1478 that the foundations of Las Palmas were laid. Stroll around the city's historic **Vegueta Quarter** to see the stamp of Spanish colonialism, from the narrow streets to ornate old buildings such as the beautiful **Casa de Colón** (Columbus's House).

Once you've had your fill of sightseeing, you can indulge in a little duty-free **shopping** in one of the many department stores, browse around the lively markets or head for the **beach** and relax on the wonderful golden sands of **Playa de las Canteras**. At the end of the day there are also numerous excellent restaurants and lively, atmospheric bars to keep you entertained for hours.

Don't Miss

*** **Cathedral of Santa Ana:** a wonderful mixture of Gothic, Baroque and neo-classical styles.
*** **Santa Ana Plaza:** Vegueta's busy main square.
*** **Columbus's House:** ornate façade with beautiful Renaissance interior.
*** **Doramas Park:** fascinating Canarian Village Museum filled with interesting ancient Canarian artefacts.

Opposite: *The cosmopolitan resort and commercial centre of Las Palmas, a city with a fascinating history.*

Las Palmas de Gran Canaria
Punta del Arrecife
Bahia del Confital
Playa de las Canteras
PLAYA IMPERIAL
TENESOYA
de Juan Réjon
La Naval
Castillo de la Luz
Puerto de la Luz
de Las Canteras
de Sagasta
MELIÁ LAS PALMAS
Albareda
Maritima del Norte
Muelle de la Luz
Puerto de la Luz
REINA ISABEL
VEROL
VILLA BLANCA
CONCORDE
de Luis
Gen. Vivés
Morote
GRAN CANARIA
SYRIA
BRAEMAR
SOL INN BARDINOS
FAYCAN
IDAFE
ROSALIA
Catalina Parque
TROCADERO
José Franchy Roca
SANSOFÉ PALACE
OLYMPIA
Santa Catalina
BAÑOSOL
ASTORIA
SOL
Fernando Guanarteme
Olof Palme
de Montevideo
Léon y Castillo
Naval Base
de Mesa y Lopez
de Mesa y Lopez
de Barcelona
M. Y. Pelayo
Club Náutico
Concepción Arenal
Blasco
Ibanez
Alcaravaneras
Playa de las Alcaravaneras
M. Gonzalez Martin
Stadium
Paseo de Chil
L. Matos
J. Antonio
M. Benitez Inglot
PIO XII
H.G. de la Torre
G. Alfonso
Maestro Valle
Escaleritas
Avenida de Las Escaleritas
L. Benitez Inglot
Joaquin Blume
Garcia Morato
Garcia Castrillo
L. de Vaga
Brazil
PIO XII
Ciudad Garden
Leopard
Doramas Parque
SANTA CATALINA
Tomas Morales
Néstor de la Torre
Casino
Monumento Léon y Castillo
Zoological Gardens
Market
Stadium
Juan XXIII
Altavista
Paseo de Chil
Léon y Castillo
Maritima del Norte
Dr. Gomez Ulla
Jimenez
Obispo
de Juan XIII
Teodoro Golfil
de Tomás Morales
de Lugo
Lugo
0
400 m
0
400 yds
SEE INSET
Monumento a Galdos
Naval Headquaters
Rabadan
Léon y Castillo
Calle de Venegas
Maritima del Norte
de Tomás Morales
Murga
MELIA CONFORT IBERIA
Cebrian
PARQUE
Bravo Murillo
Bravo Murillo
San Telmo Chapel
Alcalde Diaz Saavedra
D.J. Navarro
Mayor de Triana
Rafael Catera
Domingo G. del Rio
de Mayo
S. Bernardo
Francisco Gourie
Triana
Church of San Francisco
Theatre
Castillo de San Francisco
Busto a Colón
Cairasco Monumento
S. Nicholas Remedios
Market
Quesada
Mon. a H. de Mendoza
Hermitage of San Antonio Abad
Juan de
Casa de Colón
Town Hall
Santa Ana Cathedral
Religious Art Museum
Castillo
Dr. Chil
Canarian Museum
Vegueta

Vegueta Quarter

A tour of Las Palmas starts to the south of the port area in the historic Vegueta Quarter of the city. The oldest and most interesting sites are to be found here and it's a delightful place to wander around.

Plaza Santa Ana ***

Several bronze statues of the legendary giant Canary Island hound guard the entrance to the Plaza Santa Ana, Vegueta's main square. The dog is a symbol which has appeared on the Las Palmas coat-of-arms since 1506, and the island is supposed to have been named after it.

Santa Ana Cathedral ***

Plaza Santa Ana is dominated by the cathedral. Building began in 1497 but was constantly interrupted over the centuries, which is reflected in the cathedral's mixture of Gothic, Baroque and neo-Classical styles.

A treasure-house of relics, the cathedral's most precious artefact is the late 15th-century **Banner of the Conquest**, said to have been embroidered by Isabella I. Other works of art include a beautiful 1641 illuminated songbook, Felipe II's gold chalice, and Bishop Verdugo's pectoral cross and his throne, wrought by the 18th-century goldsmith, José Eugenio.

Diocesan Museum of Sacred Arts *

This museum is housed in the cathedral and has a wonderful collection of **Aztec** and pre-Columbian treasures, rare paintings and tapestries as well as religious artefacts and sculptures. Open 09:00–14:00, 16:00–18:00 Mon–Fri, 09:00–14:00 Sat. Closed on Sunday.

> **FEATURES OF THE CASA DE COLON**
>
> The rooms of the Casa de Colón (Columbus's House) are large and airy, with high ceilings, small windows and huge doors. The interior design is spectacularly ornate, with impressive hardwood ceilings, great cedar beams, carved embellishments and finely panelled doors.
> As in this case, many early colonial buildings were also constructed with a large gateway, with huge, heavy doors, through which the occupier could drive his carriage directly into the courtyard. This gave access to an integral carriage-house built into the main structure. Often these large doors were not conventionally hinged, instead suspended on a peg-and-eye device made from iron.

Below: *The boat-filled marina at Las Palmas. The city is still a vital seaport.*

Above: *Casa de Colón, a superb example of early Renaissance Canarian architecture.*

'FLAMENCO' ART

The many churches of Gran Canaria and the four western islands contain some superb examples of ancient religious artistry, carvings, tapestries and statuary. Almost all of these treasures, dating from the 16th–17th centuries, were carved, painted, or woven by the great Flemish masters of Gothic ecclesiastical art. The reason for the proliferation of religious artworks in the five islands was that these islands were the producers of sugar and molasses, among the most expensive commodities in Europe at that time.
So, when sugar and its by-products were shipped to the Low Countries, the Flemish master craftsmen exchanged their religious artistry for the coveted cargoes.

In the **Plaza Santa Ana** there are also a number of other buildings of historic interest: the **Bishop's Palace**, the **Herreria**, **Casa de Los Hildagos** (the House of the Nobles) and the **Regent's House**. Palms line each side of the square, and the Colonial-style **Town Hall** (*ayuntamiento*), facing the cathedral, flies three flags: of Spain, Las Palmas and the flag of the Canaries. During the **Corpus Christi festival**, the square is beautifully decorated with a fantastic carpet of flowers.

Canarian Museum ★★

To the south of Plaza Santa Ana on Calle Dr Verneau is the Canarian Museum. The most important exhibits are those dealing with the ancient Canarians. There are Cro-Magnon skulls and fascinating examples of mummified Guanches, ceramics, tools, and weapons. A huge library of books dates back to the 15th century. The natural history and botanical section is also well worth a look. Open 10:00–17:00 Monday–Friday; 10:00–13:00 Saturday and 10:00–14:00 Sunday, tel: (928) 31 56 00. Closed on holidays.

Casa de Colón ★★★

Head towards the sea from the rear of the cathedral and turn into a narrow street-cum-square to find one of the best examples of early Canarian architecture. Although named Columbus's House (Casa de Colón), it is highly unlikely that Columbus actually lived here – he probably just visited for a few days in 1492. This mansion, with its ornate façade and beautiful Renaissance interior, dates from the end of the 15th century and was the home of the first Canarian governor. Today it has an interesting museum which recreates the Age of Discovery, complete with navigational aids, models and maps. The Casa de Colón also houses the **Provincial Archives** and **Fine Arts Museum**, with a portrait of Christopher Columbus as well as interesting works by Baroque artists Veronese, Divino Morales and Guido Reni. Some artwork has been donated by the **Prado Museum** in Madrid. Open 09:30–17:30 Monday–Friday and 09:30–13:00 on Saturday, closed Sunday and holidays, tel: (928) 31 12 55.

Hermitage of San Antonio Abad **

Just across the small, cobbled square from the Casa de Colón is the delightful, creeper-draped church where Columbus is thought to have prayed before setting off. The existing building dates mainly from 1796, and was restored in 1892 in order to commemorate Columbus's voyage 400 years before.

TRIANA DISTRICT

A dual carriageway separates the Vegueta Quarter from the city proper. Directly across the busy motorway from the Antonio Abad Square or Plaza is the main shopping thoroughfare of the Triana district of the city, the Calle Mayor de Triana, a predominantly pedestrianized zone with a wealth of gorgeous Art Nouveau buildings.

Plaza de Colón *

West of the Calle Mayor de Triana is the pretty Plaza de Colón, dominated by the **Church of San Francisco** and a fine statue of Columbus. To the south of this square are two more monuments to local heroes.

Pérez Galdós Theatre **

In the eastern corner of Triana district, between the promenade and Triana Street, is the Pérez Galdós Theatre, built in 1919. Home to the theatre and opera, this impressive Modernist building is named after the local novelist, **Benito Pérez Galdós**. There are murals by Néstor de la Torre in the foyer. Galdós's house, which is now a museum, is in Calle Caño nearby.

San Telmo Church *

Continuing east on Triana Street, by the Parque San Telmo, is the San Telmo Church which dates back to the 15th century. There's also a delightfully decorated **Art Nouveau** coffee kiosk, as well as the old army building from where General Franco announced his coup d'état on 18 July 1936. The main bus station is nearby, on the seaward side of the Avenida Maritima.

THE ARTS IN LAS PALMAS

The Pérez Galdós Theatre, sponsored by the island's *cabildo* (council), is host to the annual Festival of Opera from February to the middle of March. **The Spring Festival of Music and Dance** is also held here from April to May. These events are attended by top performers from around the world. The Gran Canaria Philharmonic Orchestra performs in the theatre regularly, as does the Las Palmas Philharmonic Orchestra.

Below: *A stunning Art Nouveau coffee kiosk adorns the corner of the Parque San Telmo.*

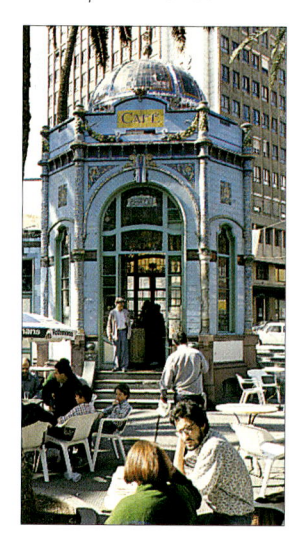

Above: Folk-dancing display at the Canarian Village, an idealized version of a traditional pueblo in Doramas Park.

Doramas Park ★★★

The Calle Mayor de Triana leads into the Calle Léon y Castillo. A few hundred metres further along is the beautiful Doramas Park, named after the last local Guanche chief.

The centrepiece of Doramas Park is the **Pueblo Canario**, a model island village that presents a rather romanticized view of Canarian society. The village was built in 1939 and was designed by the Canarian painter, **Néstor de la Torre**. This charming Canarian village has a museum that features many of De la Torre's best paintings. The museum is frequently used to stage traditional dance and music presentations. There are dancing displays on Thursday evenings. Open 10:00–13:00 Monday–Friday, 09:30–13:00 Saturday.

Further towards the port area of La Luz is the **Garden City** district, so-called because of the number of tree-lined avenues and streets dividing the residential area. Beyond the Garden City, fronting the **Alcaravanares** district, is the large **Nautical Club**, yacht basin and Naval Headquarters.

Santa Catalina ★

The next district north is the Santa Catalina area, heralded by the Santa Catalina Square. Here is the city centre proper. The **Tourist Office**, souvenir and craft market are located on the square. Duty-free shops cram the streets of Santa Catalina. There is a thriving open-air market on Sundays in the Santa Catalina Quarter of the city, called the **Mercado del Puerto**, facing the port area.

PUERTO DE LA LUZ

Named the 'Port of the Light' after the 16th-century fortress, the **Castillo de la Luz**, standing opposite one of the port's five piers, the **Muelle Pesquero**, is Europe's largest dock.

Because of its importance to Atlantic trade, this has become one of the world's most significant harbours. The present port was constructed in the late 19th century and expanded into the vast commercial area that it is now during the 20th century. The island's large fishing fleet is also based in this port.

Playa de la Canteras **

To the west of this narrow, peninsula-shaped neck of land is the beach of Las Palmas, Playa de la Canteras. Four kilometres (2½ miles) of fine white sand fronts the promenade, which is a typical town beach resort with bistros, hotels, nightclubs and even English-style pubs. The **Castillo de la Luz** fortress at the port's entrance in the La Isleta suburb is also worth a visit. Built in 1494 to repel pirate attacks, it is now home to an art gallery.

LAS PALMAS SHOPPING

Gran Canaria, and particularly Las Palmas, is a fun shopping area, not only for the selection of goods available, but more significantly, for the lack of import taxes, Spanish tax and the duty-free status of the island. The port area is always good for bargains, as are the shops along Calle Mayor de Triana and Calle Mesa y Lopez. Visit the **El Corte Inglés** department store, which is open all day and is stocked full of goods, or the **Galerías Preciados** for real bargains. They are both in Triana.

Municipal Market *

The Municipal Market (Mercado Central), in the Vegueta Quarter, is a must for lovers of the bustle of stall life and bargaining for traditional fare. Fresh and cured fish; fresh, cooked and preserved meats; cheeses from all over the islands; flowers; vegetables; herbs; spices; fruit and other local goods are rather temptingly displayed here.

Santa Catalina Park **

Usually a mass of colourful stalls, Santa Catalina Park bustles with life, where everything from leatherwork to postcards can be bought. You may even find a real bargain.

> **EL RASTRO**
>
> Visit **Santa Catalina Park**, in the centre of town, on Sunday morning. The entire plaza becomes a fascinating flea market, the **Rastro**, with more than 250 stalls. The market opens at roughly 09:00 and closes at 14:30. All around the square are cafés and bistros where you can relax and decide which stalls to visit before joining the melee. Everything from tacky souvenirs to leather goods, ceramics, craftwork, flowers and plants, second-hand items, antiques and books are hawked here. A variety of snacks, tapas and refreshments are on hand, and after a morning's browsing and buying, you can take a horse-drawn taxi carriage (*tartana*) to your favourite restaurant or back to the hotel.

Below: *Triana, a shopper's paradise for duty-free goods at bargain prices.*

Las Palmas at a Glance

BEST TIMES TO VISIT

The Canary Islands are ideal all year round for the sunny weather they always seem to offer. From the end of **October** to the end of **April** is generally considered the High Season. Many of the tourists from Europe book in advance for the months from **November** to **February** and note that the Christmas period is especially popular.

GETTING THERE

Most visitors from abroad, apart from those from the Spanish mainland, arrive by air at **Gando International Airport**, halfway between the capital and the south coast resorts. There are **ferry services** from Cádiz in Spain to Las Palmas for both passengers and cars. Arrange these sort of transfers when you are booking your accommodation.

GETTING AROUND

Apart from taking organized **coach tours**, taking local **bus services**, or private **taxi** excursions in the island, the **hire-car** system is probably the best way to see this island's sights. If you bring your own car, however, you must bear in mind the following stipulations: you must have a valid driving licence, an International Driving Permit, a Green Card Insurance, a Vehicle Registration Document, a Bail Bond, a spare set of light bulbs, a red triangle warning sign, a change of headlights system and, of course, your passport. Main roads throughout the entire archipelago are excellent.

WHERE TO STAY

Hotels and accommodation in Las Palmas is varied as in most major cities around the world. Most hotels offer the usual facilities, some without a swimmimg pool and extra luxuries, like the **Parque Hotel**, located in the old city area, the **Rosalina**, a 3-star hotel between Catalina Park and the beach, and the **Iberia Sol Hotel**, not on the beach, but with excellent sea aspects. Apart from the beach-side hotels, the plusher hotels offering all ameneties, including a pool, are the **Santa Catalina** (host to the British and Spanish Royal families), **Mélia Cristina**, **Reina Isabel**, the **Concorde**, and **Sol Inn Bardinos**, the city's tallest hotel. A variety of apartment blocks are also available.

LUXURY
Melia Cristiana, Calle Gomera 6; tel: (928) 36 64 54, fax: 26 84 11; designed for high-spending businessmen.
Reina Isabel, Calle Alfredo L Jones 40; tel: (928) 26 01 00, fax: 27 45 58; close to Canteras Beach.
Santa Catalina, Parque Doramas, Calle León y Castillo 277; tel: (928) 24 30 40, fax: 24 27 64; in Doramas Park.

MID-RANGE
Sol Inn Bardinos, Calle Eduardo Benot 3; tel: (928) 26 61 00, fax: 22 91 39; a short walk from Catalina Park, Canteas beach and the port.
Concorde, Tomas Miller 85; tel: (928) 26 27 50, fax: 26 57 74; centrally located in the Santa Catalina district.
Melia Confort Iberia, Maritime Avenue-North; tel: (928) 36 11 33, fax: 36 13 44; on the seafront, not far from Alcaravaneras beach and the Nautical Club.
Imperial Playa, Calle Ferreras 1; tel: (928) 26 48 54, fax: 46 94 42; wide range of facilities, situated on Canteras beach.

BUDGET
Atlanta, Calle Alfredo L Jones 37; tel: (928) 22 26 71, fax: 27 34 85; located on Canteras beach with basic facilities.
Bajamar, Calle Venezuela 34; tel: (928) 27 62 54, fax: 27 62 54; Hotel apartments located a short distance from Paseo and main beach.
Gran Canaria, Paseo de Las Canteras; tel: (928) 27 50 78, fax: 26 24 20; fine location on Canteras beach with good facilities.
Parque, Muelle de Las Palmas 2; tel: (928) 36 80 00; efficient, business-like, situated between the old and new districts.
Olympia, Dr Grau Bassas 1, DP 35007; tel: (928) 26 17 20, fax: 26 26 17; centrally located and near bus transport.

Las Palmas at a Glance

Where to Eat

Las Palmas is renowned for its incredible variety of eating places, from a mock steamboat, **The Mississippi**, moored in the Sporting Marina, to the eighth-floor luxury restaurant in the **Hotel Reina Isabel**. There are also Japanese and **Chinese**, **Russian** or **Lebanese** restaurants, **tapas bars** and **bistros**. There are several vegetarian restaurants in the city, and even one serving typically British fare. For succulent food the following come highly recommended:

El Novillo Precoz, Calle Portugal 9; tel: (928) 22 16 59; behind Playas Canteras with Argentinian-style meat dishes.
Casa Julio, Calle Naval 123; tel: (928) 46 01 39; Canarian and fish dishes located in port sector. Closed Sunday.
Pasta Real, Calle Secretario Padilla 28; tel: (928) 26 22 67; not strictly Canarian, but this is where to find some of the city's best pasta and delicious vegetarian dishes.

Shopping

Las Palmas is a mecca for shoppers with goods at duty-free prices. August is best for the sales and prices of watches, cameras, electrical goods, perfumes, wines, tobacco etc. are often lower than in resort shops. The port area and both **Calle Mayor de Lopez** are good for bargains. The **El Corte Ingles** store is open all day and the **Glaerias Preciados** are worth a visit. The Municipal Market, or **Mercado Central**, in Vegueta Quarter, is a bustle of stall life with bargaining for traditional fare. Fresh and cured fish, fresh, cooked and preserved meats, cheeses from the islands, flowers, vegetables, herbs, spices, fruit and other local goods are displayed here. There is a thriving open-air market on Sundays in the Santa Catalina Quarter called the **Mercado del Puerto**, facing the port. Santa Catalina Park is a mass of colourful stalls selling local souvenirs, ranging from leatherwork to needlework and postcards. Open 09:00–13:00, 16:00–20:00 Monday–Friday. In the summer months, many shops stay open all morning from 08:00–14:00 and often late into the night on festival and holidays.

Tours and Excursions

Tourist buses and some taxi companies offer a variety of tours. The Tourist Office on Catalina Park has leaflets on tours both in the city and to the island's interior. Tours include the Vegueta quarter; main shopping areas; the Canario Museum, the Canarian Village in Doramas Park and the nearby Néstor Museum. There are many options, both day and night, from the **Grand Tour** of the interior and the **Jeep Safari** to the mountains, to the **Scala Cabaret** and **Casino** night, or the Wild West night at **Sioux City**. You can also take a trip to **Morocco** in North Africa for a day's sightseeing and shopping.

Useful Contacts

Tourist Board, Parque Santa Catalina, Las Palmas; tel: (928) 26 46 23 or (928) 27 16 00.
Patronado de Turismo, Léon y Castillo 17, Las Palmas; tel: (928) 36 24 22 / 36 26 22. Fax: (928) 36 28 22.
Council of Tourism and Transport, Plaza de los Detechos Humanos, s/n Edificio Usos Multiples, 6th and 7th Floors, 35003 Las Palmas; tel: (928) 36 16 00/ 36 11 56. fax: (928) 38 06 16.
Aeropuerto de Gando, tel: (928) 25 41 40.
IBERIA Airlines, Avenida Ramirez Béthancourt, Las Palmas; tel: (928) 37 02 22.

EAST CANARY ISLANDS	J	F	M	A	M	J	J	A	S	O	N	D
AVERAGE TEMP. °C	16	17	17	18	19	20	23	23	21	21	18	17
AVERAGE TEMP. °F	61	63	63	64	66	68	73	73	70	70	64	63
HOURS OF SUN DAILY	7	7	8	8	9	9	10	8	8	8	7	6
DAYS OF RAINFALL	7	6	5	4	2	1	1	1	2	6	10	9
RAINFALL mm	36	8	2	11	2	-	-	-	6	3	58	9
RAINFALL in	1.5	0	0	0.5	0	0	0	0	0	0	2	0

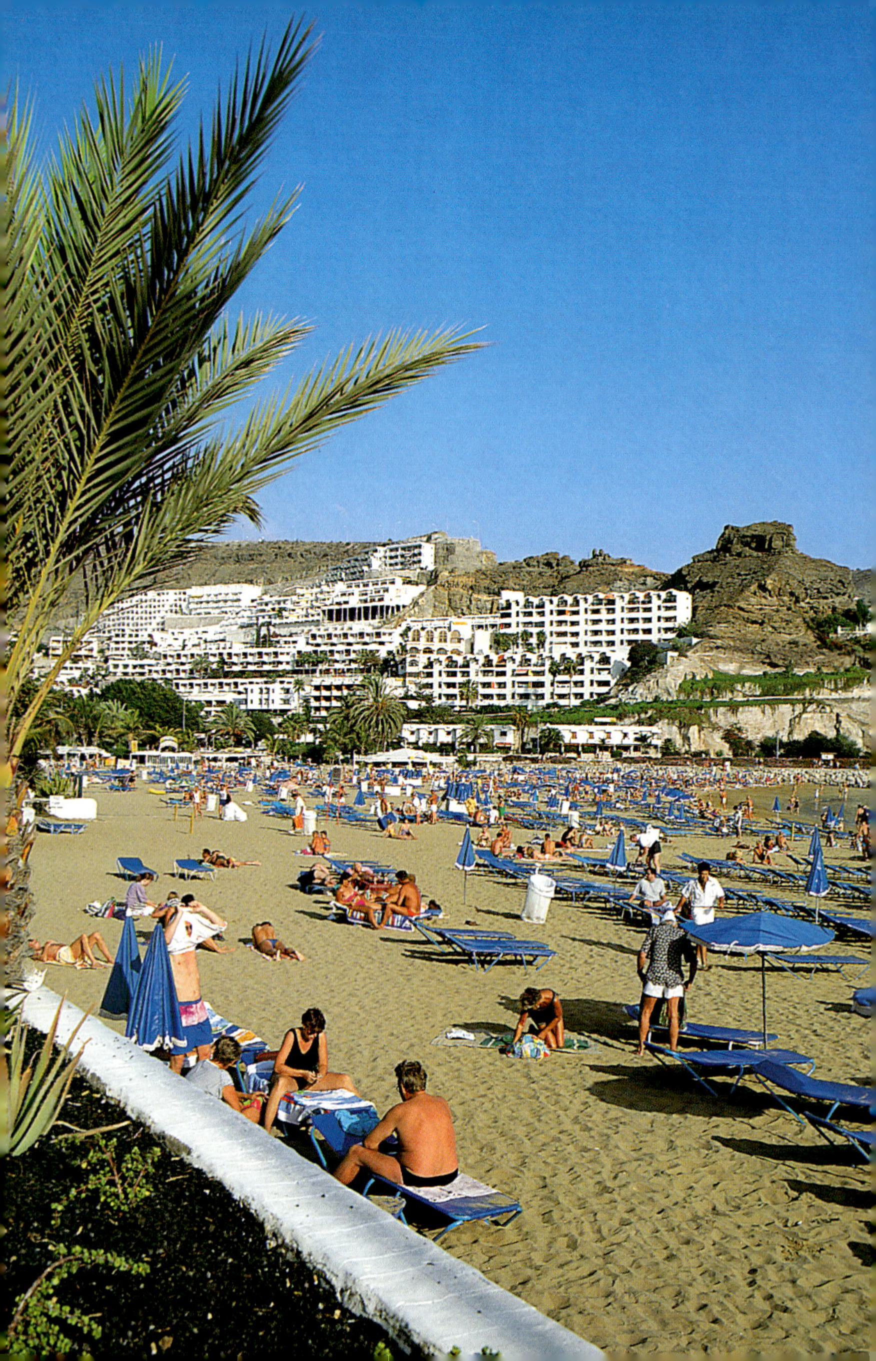

3
Gran Canaria

Lying almost at the heart of the Canary archipelago, Gran Canaria is a fascinating island: an exhilarating blend of old and new. Most visitors head for its superb sandy beaches, attracted by the year-round sun, superb watersports and hectic nightlife. The capital, **Las Palmas**, is another big draw; a sophisticated, cosmopolitan city packed with beautiful old buildings and excellent for shopping.

Yet beyond the beaches lies an eye-catching natural wonderland virtually unscathed by modern development and preserving centuries-old culture within its domain. Gran Canaria is known as a 'continent in miniature' because of its tremendously varied terrain. Arid deserts, rugged mountains and rocky gorges contrast with lush tropical forests, banana plantations, vineyards and sugar canes. Scattered throughout the interior are charming whitewashed villages and ancient archaeological sites, relics of the long vanished Guanche civilization.

Gando International Airport is situated on the east coast, almost midway between Las Palmas to the north and the **Maspalomas** resort on the southeast coast. An excellent motorway runs down the east side of the island and a secondary road circumnavigates Gran Canaria, with winding routes linking the picturesque towns and villages in the interior. Whether you wish to soak up the sun, shop till you drop, explore the island's breathtaking scenery or discover its historic past, Gran Canaria is the perfect place for a wonderful holiday.

DON'T MISS

*** **Telde:** original capital, nearby Cuatro Puertas, ancient Guanche site.
*** **Teror:** 16th-century basilica and sanctuary of the Virgin of the Pines.
*** **Aldea Valley** and **Aldea Mirador:** spectacular east coast views.
*** **Gáldar:** historic site, fascinating painted cave with Guanche pictographs.
** **Ingenio:** oldest village on island, lace-making centre and Stone Museum.

Opposite: *The lovely, sheltered beach of Puerto Rico, excellent for watersports.*

42   GRAN CANARIA

GRAN CANARIA'S WILD, WEST

Experience the theatrical thrills of staged gunfights, bank-robbing, knife-throwing, lassooing and lynchings at **Sioux City** near San Agustín. This Wild West theme park looks just like a spaghetti western film set. Try to catch one of the shows (12:00 and 18:00), or go to the barbecues, Wed and Sat at 20:00. Tel: (928) 76 25 73.

THE COASTAL RESORTS

Apart from the 4km-long (2½ mile) **Canteras Beach** to the west of Las Palmas, there are three other major resorts on the southern coast of the island, which could almost be called the Costa Canaria since it has so much in common with the costas on the Spanish mainland. The resorts are places you'll either love or hate. Both **Playa de Inglés** and **Maspalomas** attract the lion's share of tourists, who come for the usual sun and fun found in beach resorts all over the world. These two conurbations have more or less merged into one long mass of high and low-rise buildings fronting a vast sandy beach, which has excellent water-sport facilities. Maspalomas also boasts **Holiday World** – a large amusement park complete with ferris wheel, dodgems and laser games. Not far west of Maspalomas is the third resort of **Puerto Rico**. South of Maspalomas is a great expanse of sand dunes which resemble a mini-Sahara, with a long, undeveloped beach running around a large headland, protected from development.

Other popular resorts along the south coast include **San Augustín**, **Arguineguín** and **Puerto del Mogán**. Many resorts are high-rise, concrete sprawls but they all have superb facilities. **Puerto del Mogán** is a lovely place, with picturesque whitewashed villas and a very smart marina. There's a string of excellent sandy beaches around the island and those on the east coast are much quieter.

Above: *The natural beauty of the sand dunes in Maspalomas is quite outstanding.*

A COASTAL TOUR

It is possible to tour around the island's coast, 245km (152 miles) long, in a full day – but you'll have to start rather early. If you take the main road south out of Las Palmas, and travel past Vegueta and the Castillo San Cristóbal, the turning for Telde will be visible. This road will take you into the town.

Telde ★★★

This is the second largest town on the island, apart from the tourist conurbations. The first colonial settlement, Telde was originally the seat of the last Guanche king, **Doramas**, and it is now divided into three districts. **San Juan** district is named after the 15th-century volcanic rock-built Church of St John the Baptist, which contains a magnificent, 500-year-old gilt-wood Flemish altarpiece, a 16th-century image of Christ created from maize cobs donated by the Tabasco Indians of Mexico, and a

---

CAVE HOUSES

Just a short distance south of Telde, in mountains sacred to the ancient Guanches, there are numerous cave dwellings. Near Cenobio de Valerón, on the Montaña del Gallego, there is a fine example of a structure known to the Guanches as a *Tagoror*. This circular building was a meeting place for the island's kings. On the Montaña de Cuatro Puertas is another ancient structure, hollowed out of rock and used in Guanche funeral rites, prior to the custom of embalming. The mountain is named after the four openings of the construction, which served as a platform for the bodies of deceased native kings thousands of years before the arrival of the Spanish.

Above: *Boats and waterfront at the picturesque resort of Puerto de Mogán.*

wonderful painting by the well-known Italian artist Vicenzo Carducci. The **San Francisco** district is named after the Convent of San Francisco, which is well known for its elaborate interior panelling. **Los Llanos** district was originally the peasant quarter, home to the Moorish and black slaves who once worked the island's sugar plantations.

Keeping on the same road, the Guanche mausoleum of **Cuatro Puertas** (the Four-Doored Mountain), can be visited just off the road to the left. Today the cave burial sites have been turned into goat pens.

Ingenio **

This was a town which was founded by the Portuguese and it has inherited a tradition of witchcraft and superstition from the large slave population which inhabited the area for a long time. Stop briefly at **Museo de Piedras e Artesania Canaria**, to see the interesting Guanche artifacts and the fascinating display of old farm tools and rocks at Ingenio which is also famous for its fine embroidery work.

If you rejoin the main road south, you'll see that the Aeroclub is indicated to the left and a short detour right will take you up into the picturesque Barranco Berriel, to the dramatic scenery of the **Aguila Canyon**. Back on the road, by-pass Playa de Inglés and Maspalomas, where you will join the beautiful coastal route with views of fine bays from **Pasito Blanco**, through to the resort area of Puerto Rico, to just before Playa de Mogán, where the steep-sided **Barranco de Mogán** channels the road inland.

A KING'S LAST STAND

In the extreme northwest corner of Gran Canaria is a weird rock formation riddled with gaunt caverns. Near the town of **Gáldar**, this site was once the centre of the realm of **Tenesor Semidan**, the Guanche king. In 1483 he was beaten by the Spanish and forcibly converted to Christianity by being baptized here. After his conversion he made peace with the Spanish and persuaded his followers to do the same.

Valley of La Aldea ★★★

The road from Mogán follows the panoramic Valley of La Aldea to a lookout, the **Mirador de Balcon** – a photographer's dream. The next stop, **El Risco**, has a pretty little beach. Frightening switchbacks pass two roadside crosses and a number of lookout sites. Stop at the **Dedo de Díos**, Finger of God mirador, just before Agaete town. Below here is the **Puerto de Las Nieves**, a banana shipping port and fishing village. Be adventurous and try one of the excellent restaurants here for a meal of locally caught, freshly prepared fish.

After lunch, pay a visit to **Agaete** to see the Hermitage of La Virgen de Las Nieves with its fine 16th-century Flemish triptych (painted panel) of the Madonna and Child. This region is perfect for cultivating fruit and vegetables. Between Agaete and Gáldar at the next stop are two sites on the right of the road: Cave of the Crosses and the Hermitage of Saint Isidro de Viejo.

Gáldar ★★★

The town of Gáldar was home to the last local chief, **Tenesor Semidan**, and has several interesting historic sites, including the ancient **Painted Cave** (Cueva Pintada), with wonderful examples of colourful, geometric Guanche designs and the **Tumulo de la Guancha**, an ancient cemetery. The Town Hall, fronted by a magnificent dragon tree, has a museum of Guanche artefacts. The 18th-century church, built on the site of Tenesor Semidan's palace, contains a 15th-century green ceramic font thought to come from Andalucia and to have been used in the forcible conversion of the indigenous inhabitants during the Spanish conquest.

After Gáldar, the road strides out over the Vega Mayor plain, from **Santa María de Guia**. This pretty village is known for its tasty goat's milk and delicious thistle-flower cheese. It also has a lovely, tiny church, with wonderful sculptures by José Lujan Pérez, who was born at nearby Tres Palmas. This quaint little village also has a connection with the French composer, Camille Saint-Saëns, who lived in Llanos de Parra, just up the road.

RAINMAKERS OF RAMA

Literally, one of the most striking festivals of the Canaries occurs during summer in Agaete, on the northwest coast of Gran Canaria. This is the festival of the Rama. So popular is the ritual that locals vary the date to keep the number of attendees down. Dating back to Guanche days, the fiesta involves locals congregating in the mountains above the town and marching to the coast armed with green boughs. Upon reaching the sea, they beat the water with branches, in the age-old ritual of invoking rain from the Gods. The procession culminates in a heaving sea of bodies celebrating Rama with music and dancing in the streets of Agaete.

CALDERA DE BANDAMA

There are superb views from the **Pico de Bandama** mirador 574m (1889ft) into this picturesque volcanic crater which is situated in the eastern corner of the island. Almost 1km (⅔ miles) across and 200m (656ft) deep, the crater is green and fertile, and has an isolated farm at its centre. Coachloads of tourists on their way to the mirador are causing the sides of the crater to erode: it's a steep, relatively short walk to the valley floor – but do your bit for conservation and stick to the path.

Below: *Gran Canaria's maritime importance was underpinned by superb natural harbours, which today cater more for pleasure boats than commercial vessels.*

Arucas **

This historic town was originally the site of the **Hermitage of San Pedro**, when Pedro Perón, the island's governor, established it in 1526. Apart from a superb **Municipal Park**, the town's main claim to fame is its early 20th-century parish church, built in neo-Gothic style, and resembling a city cathedral.

Up on a hill here, a botanical garden and mirador has been laid out for views over the fertile valley and plain.

Teror ***

Instead of returning to Las Palmas via the coastal road, take a detour into the mountains up to the elegant town of Teror. It is a small, northern town with lovely wide streets lined with colonial houses. It was here, in 1481, that the Madonna was said to have appeared in a pine tree, establishing the town as a centre of pilgrimage. Notable sites in the town include the 18th-century, neo-Classical-style **Nuestra Señora del Pino** basilica and jewelled shrine, the 18th-century neo-Gothic tower and the Bishop's Palace.

A MOUNTAIN TOUR

This could be either a day or half-day tour, depending on the time spent at each site. This tour takes the visitor across the crown of the island, where you will see five important inland sites.

Viera y Clavijo Jardín Canario ***

Take the road out of Las Palmas along the motorway between the Vegueta and Triana districts. The road leads up to the Viera y Clavijo Jardín Canario, a spectacular botanical garden. This garden has a magnificent collection

A MOUNTAIN TOUR

> **HONEYCOMB HILL**
>
> In northwest Gran Canaria a volcanic mass known as the **Cuesta de Silva** stands near Santa María de Guía. One mountain face, called the **Cenobio de Valerón**, is a great arc of stone, overhung by a steep ledge. High up, and apparently inaccessible, numerous small caves have been carved out of the cliff face by the Guanches. Modern steps now lead up to the caverns. Wooden doors once covered the caves' entrances, and historians dispute as to whether they were utilized as grain silos, or if they were pre-marital refuges for eligible native maidens.

of flora on show including the dragon trees and cactus garden. Continue up through the narrow part of Tafira and follow the signs to the golf course perched on top of the volcanic crater of the same name.

Above: *Villages sheltered by mountains are a typical sight in the rugged interior.*
Below: *The Cruz de Tejeda, a popular vantage point overlooking magnificent natural scenery.*

Santa Brígida **

Returning to the main road, the next stop is Santa Brígida town. Once known as Sataute, or Little Palm Tree, this typical Canarian agricultural town, surrounded by palms, stands on the brink of a ravine. The church contains a lovely sculpture of Christ by a local artist. The town is also famous for its wonderful pottery work.

Vega de San Mateo *

If you do this tour on a Saturday or Sunday, don't miss the fruit and flower market in the next village, Vega de San Mateo. The local markets are open in the mornings. Take a walk around it to see what the people like to eat.

Cross of Tejeda **

From here, the road winds up, with two fine miradors on the right hand side, to the summit of the main route, the Cruz, or Cross of Tejeda at 1450m (4757ft). A National Parador hotel is located here.

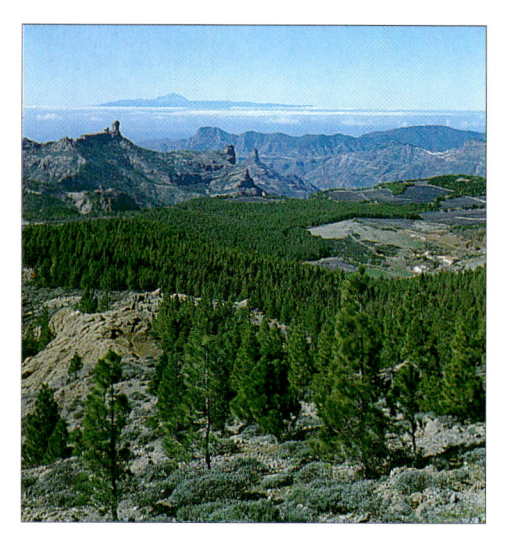

Above: Spectacular panoramas abound in the interior. Here, pine forests are backed by Roque Nubio.

Roque Nubio ★★

The spectacular pinnacle of the Roque Nubio (Cloud Rock), 1817m (5961ft) high, rises magnificently from the bleak volcanic landscape. Look out for the huge boulders named **El Fraile** (The Monk) and **Roque Bentaiga**. In the distance, you will be able to see the outline of the spectacular Teide mountain on nearby Tenerife, to the west. From the road here, take the side route up to the island's peak, the 1949m-high (6394ft) **Pico de las Nieves**, for breathtaking views.

Artenara ★★

Back at Tejeda Parador, make another detour to the west. This side road leads around the peak of **Moriscos**, at 1771m (5810ft), to the isolated village of Artenara, nestled in countryside surrounded by cave-riddled gorges and cross-crowned peaks. The main attaction here is the small hermitage known as the **Cueva de la Virgen**, a shrine cut out of the volcanic rock.

There is a fine panoramic view from the **Mirador la Silla** here, and in the distance, to the northwest, is the peak of Tamadaba Mountain, 1444m (4738ft) high and surrounded by the forests of the Pinar de Tamadaba. Returning to the Parador, it will probably be time for lunch, which you should have before setting off on the spectacular drive through the island's highest mountains. Leave room for a dessert so that you can sample some of the island's finest in the next village.

The road south from the Parador leads through the village of **Tejeda**, renowned for its delicious cakes. The route now winds precariously around the Cloud Rock to the right, and across the Barranco de Ayacate, with breathtaking views of the **Pico de las Nieves** to the left.

TROGLODYTES

Just northwest of Tejeda is one of the most charming villages on Gran Canaria, **Artenara**. Most of its dwellings are carved out of the precipitous volcanic rock. Set in pine forests, Artenara is built into the mountainside and is the island's highest village. Even the church, **La Virgen de la Cuevita** (of the Little Cave), melts into the rockface, surmounted by a tiny bell tower. Look for door number nine. This will lead you through the mountainside to a ledge which has been transformed into a cliff-side restaurant.

San Bartolomé de Tirajana ★★★

Just before entering the town of San Bartolomé de Tirajana, the landscape is dotted with caves, notably those of **Del Pinar** and the **Cuevas Blancas**. Known in Guanche times as Tamaran, San Bartolomé de Tirajana is built in the vast crater of Tirajana, under the shadow of the central massif of the island. The final vestiges of Guanche were routed here by the conquistador **Pedro de Vera**, who laid siege to the last natives until they starved. The surrealistic landscape here is covered with trees, orchards and almond groves interspersed with pine, cherry and plum trees mixed with palms. This is the most visited attraction in the entire Canaries, and the views from the **Mirador Posador** are certainly exceptional. The Posador is a small hotel which bakes its own bread in an ancient traditional oven. From here a road leads directly south, through the marvellously picturesque **Fataga Ravine**, down to the coast at Maspalomas.

> **BARRANCO VEGETATION**
>
> A *barranco* is a generally dried up riverbed, either founded by twisted lava beds, or carved out by the forces of nature into a steep sided gorge. There are several notable barrancos on Gran Canaria, often much greener than you'd expect. Apart from palms and pines, of which the endemic species is *Pinus canariensis*, look for the finger-like succulent, *Euphorbia canariensis*, the pink rock-rose, *Cistus symphytifolius*, and the primordial vegetation, Aeonium. The dwarf yellow broom, *Teline microphylla*, is prevelant, as are clumps of balos bushes.

Santa Lucía ★★

From San Bartolomé you can either take the Fataga road, or head for the east coast along the main road which runs through **Santa Lucía** village. Apart from Santa Lucía's delightful white-washed church, the village has an ethnological museum which, as well as exhibiting many fascinating artifacts of Guanche life and death, and a collection of mummies, also houses a typical 17th-century Canarian room. The **Museum La Fortaleza**, contained in a mock fort, also has a restaurant, and Guanche artefacts provide an atmospheric backdrop to a typically Canarian meal. There are some artisan shops in Santa Lucía which are worth visiting.

Temisas ★

As the road leaves Santa Lucía, the **Fortaleza Grande** is visible just off to the right. Temisas, to the left, is a renowned olive-producing area. Between here and the next village, the road is chiselled through the red rock, and some exciting Guanche remains have been excavated in the **Balos** and **Guayadeque** gorges near here.

Below: *Vintage transport still navigates the treacherous mountain roads.*

Gran Canaria at a Glance

BEST TIMES TO VISIT

Winter is the favourite time to visit Gran Canaria for most Europeans, although this is the busiest time of the year. British visitors arrive all year round as a suntan is almost guaranteed and the waters are warm enough to swim comfortably. The climate in the south of the island is generally better than that in the north.

GETTING THERE

Most visitors from abroad, except those from the Spanish mainland, arrive by air at **Gando International Airport**, just south of the capital. There are **ferry services** from Cádiz in Spain for passengers and cars to Las Palmas.

GETTING AROUND

Car hire is the most popular way of getting around the island. Apart from hiring a car and doing your own thing, there are an enormous number of **coach tours** which can be joined at hotels or pre-designated pick-up points. Should you bring your own **car** on the ferry, make sure you have the right documents, drive on the right and wear seat belts, which are compulsory.

WHERE TO STAY

Many visitors to the islands opt for **apartment accommodation**, and Gran Canaria has a huge choice of apartment blocks, not only in Las Palmas, but in the resort areas of Playa del Inglés, Bahia Feliz, Puerto Rico, Maspalomas, San Agustin and Arguineguin or Patalavaca.

Agaete
BUDGET
Princess Guayarmina, Los Berrazales; tel: (928) 89 80 09, fax: 89 85 25; basic facilities but with a swimming pool.

Arucas
MID-RANGE
Bella Arehucas, Calle Panchito Hernandez 10; tel: (928) 60 06 51; beautiful and convenient location for touring.

San Agustin
LUXURY
Melia Tamarindos, Calle Retamas 3; tel: (928) 77 40 90, fax: 77 40 91; superior facilities in excellent location.

MID-RANGE
Ifa Beach Hotel, Los Jazamines 25; tel: (928) 76 51 00, fax: 76 85 99; one of the best-priced accommodation options in this region with good pool.

BUDGET
Inter Club Atlantis, Los Jazamines 2; tel: (928) 76 09 50, fax: 76 09 74; reasonably priced, good facilities, pool.

San Bartolomé de Tirijana
LUXURY
Folias, Calle Las Retamas 17; tel: (928) 76 24 50; basic facilities but good location.

MID-RANGE
Beverly Park, Hamburgo 2 (Playa del Ingles); tel: (928) 76 17 50, fax: 76 18 12; good location; golf course and pool.

Playa del Inglés
LUXURY
Apolo, Avenida Estados Unidos 28; tel: (928) 76 00 58, fax: 76 3918; excellent range of facilities plus swimming pool.
Las Margeritas, Avenida Gran Canaria 38; tel: (928) 76 11 12, fax: 76 53 80; wide range of facilities and swimming pool.
Lucana, Plaza del Sol 1; tel: (928) 77 40 40, fax: 77 41 41; perfect location with good pool and wide range of facilities.

MID-RANGE
Rey Carlos, Avenida Tirijana 14; tel: (928) 76 01 16, fax: 76 29 45; good position, pool and range of services.
Continental, Avenida de Italia 2; tel: (928) 76 16 05, fax: 77 14 84; a medium-size hotel for this kind of resort, with a good pool.
Wakiki, Avenida de Gran Canaria 20; tel: (928) 76 23 00; good location and wide range of facilities for price, pool.

BUDGET
Ifa Regina Mar, Avenida EE. UU. 38; tel: (928) 76 76 16, fax: 76 51 67; good price for this fairly basic hotel, good pool.

Maspalomas
LUXURY
Iberotel Maspalomas Oasis, Playa de Maspalomas, tel: (928) 76 01 70, fax: 14 11 92; the top hotel on this resort, all facilities.

MID-RANGE
Ifa Faro, Playa de Maspalomas; tel: (928) 14 22 14, fax: 14 19 40;

Gran Canaria at a Glance

rather limited facilities and services, but good pool.
Palm Beach, Avenida del Oasis s/n; tel: (928) 76 29 20, fax: 14 18 08; a sophisticated hotel.

BUDGET
Green Golf Apartments, Campo de Golf; tel: (928) 77 39 49; facilities for children, 3 pools.
Riu Palace Meloneras, Playa de Maspalomas; tel: (928) 14 31 82; short walk from beach.

Puerto de Mogán
MID-RANGE
Guest House Silene, Tomas Zerolo 9; tel: (928) 33 01 99; convenient to local facilities, homely atmosphere.

Puerto Rico
LUXURY
Revoli, Avenida del Mogán; tel: (928) 56 12 58, fax: 56 20 96; best facilities in this resort.

MID-RANGE
Rio Sol, Cornisa 24; tel: (928) 74 51 48, fax: 56 07 74; apartments with pool.

WHERE TO EAT

San Agustín
San Agustín Beach Club, tel: (928) 76 04 00; seafood.
Chez Mario, Los Pinos, s/n, San Bartolome de Tirijana; tel: (928) 76 18 17; inexpensive Italian dishes, pleasant surroundings.

Playa del Inglés
Meson Viuda de Franco, Avda. Tirijana 2; tel: (928) 76 03 71; international specialities.

Bali, Avenida Bonn 23, tel: (928) 76 32 61; good Indonesian fare.

Also in the South
Las Cumbres, Avenida Tirijana 9; tel: (928) 76 09 41; varied international menu.
Casa del Abuelo, Calle Alfereces Provisionales 11; tel: (928) 76 44 11; local fare.

Tejeda
El Refugio, Cruz de Tejeda; tel: (928) 66 61 88; terrace service.

Arguineguín
Restaurant del Mar; harbour views, excellent fare.

Telde
Pablo Silva, Calle General de El Goro 1; tel: (928) 57 46 82; fine Canarian dishes.
La Pardilla, Calle Raimundo Lulio 54, tel: (928) 69 51 02; Canarian and International fare.

Tafira Alta
La Masia de Canarias, Calle Murillo 36; tel: (928) 35 01 20; excellent Canarian food.

TOURS AND EXCURSIONS

There are numerous options for organized or individual tours. Many independent **coach** companies offer various trips from one hour to full-day outings. Hotels display a selection of organized tours with guides, or an official **Tourist Board** can recommend a number of alternatives such as the North Africa Tour to Morocco. Several tour operators offer day-long excursions which fly you to the village of El-Aaiun for its fascinating camel market, souks and typical Moroccan way of life.
Donkey or **camel safaris:** Safaris, Carretera de Faro de Maspalomas.
Deep-sea fishing: Club Nautico Metropole, Paseo Alonso Quesada; tel: (928) 24 43 46.
Flying, parachuting, sky-diving: Aeroclub Maspalomas, tel: (928) 76 24 47.
Golf: Campo de Golf de Maspalomas, Avenida de Africa; tel: (928) 76 25 81.
Sailing: Escuela Territorial de Vela de Puerto Rico, Calle Doreste, Puerto Rico; tel: (928) 56 07 72.
Watersports: Sun Club, Playa del Inglés; tel: (928) 76 09 50.
Casablanca, Marrakesh or **Agadir:** Guillermo Sintes Reyes SA. Calle Artemi Semidan 11, 3rd Floor, Las Palmas, tel: (928) 27 71 53, 27 72 08 or 27 41 14.

USEFUL CONTACTS

Tourist Board, Parque Santa Catalina, Las Palmas; tel: (928) 26 46 23 or 27 16 00.
Tourist Office, Playa del Inglés, Ave. de España; tel: (928) 77 15 50
Patronado de Turismo, Léon y Castille 17, Las Palmas; tel: (928) 36 24 22, fax: 36 28 22.
Council of Tourism and Transport, Plaza de los Detechos Humanos, s/n Edificio Usos Multiples, 6th and 7th Floors, 35003 Las Palmas, tel: (928) 36 16 00/ 36 11 56. fax: (928) 38 06 16.

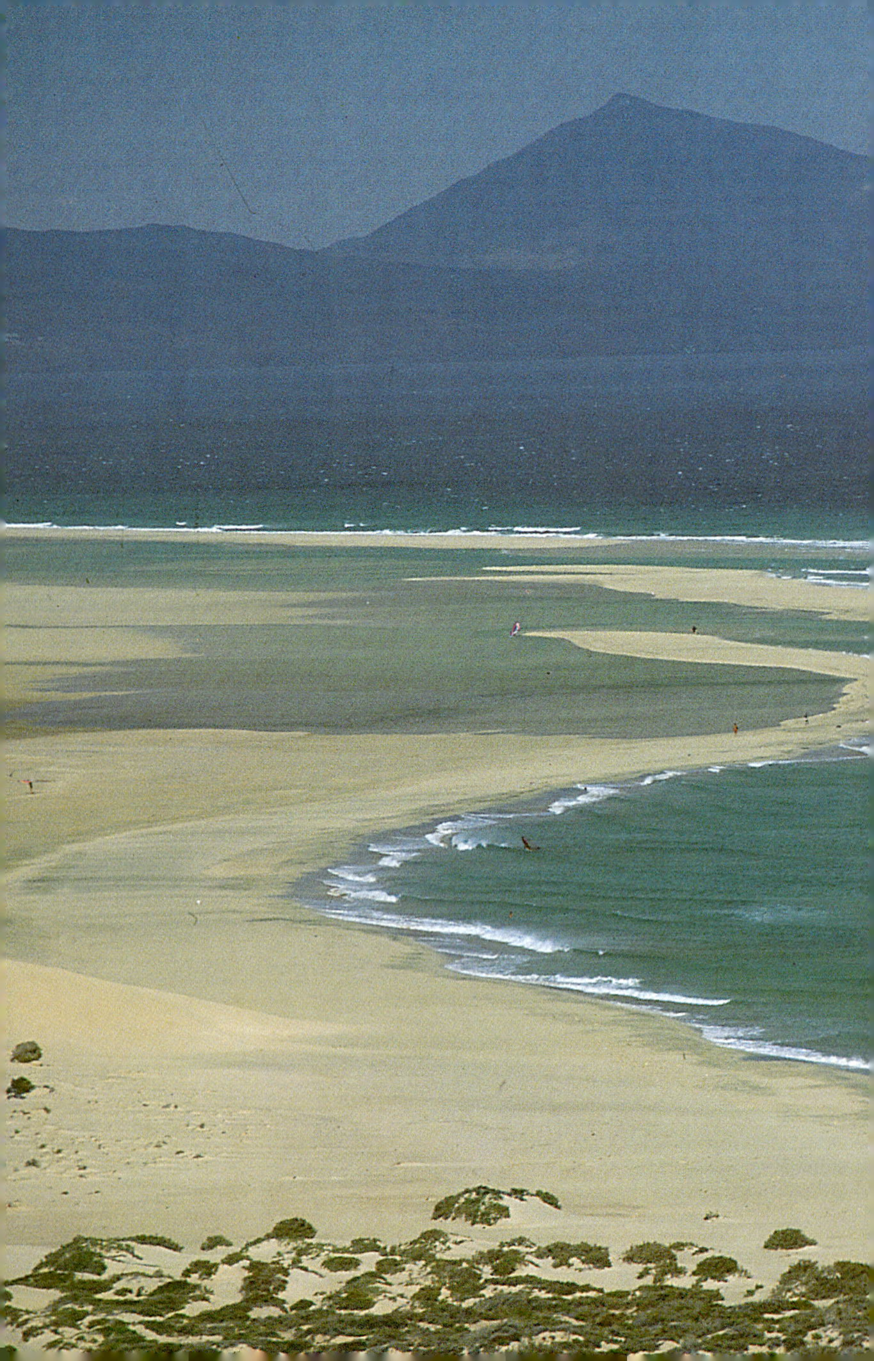

4
Fuerteventura

Fuerteventura is the largest of the Canary Islands after Tenerife and is arid and desert-like. It is known as the '**Viejo Pais Canario**', or the 'Old Country', as it echoes the conditions of its mother country, Africa, just 90km (56 miles) to the east. The countryside has been denuded by both man and goat, and, with little rainfall, the island is practically devoid of vegetation and has a tiny population. It is rather stark and bare but it does have some of the most glorious beaches – miles and miles of lovely, soft sand. It can get a bit windy at times but for the avid windsurfer this is the ideal place to visit!

Terracing, windmills, and jealously guarded water collection pools enable the locals to wrest a meagre crop of maize, alfalfa, wheat, barley, chick peas, pineapples and a few vegetables from the cindery and sandy soil. The many goats and chickens provide meat, but some Fuerteventurans turn to the sea for its abundant harvest.

With the longest coastline of the Canary group, the island stretches over 100km (62 miles) in length. It is this beautiful coastline that attracts the visitors who select the island for its isolation, tranquility and perfect beaches. The island is divided into two – the bulbous, **northern** two-thirds, with its historic sites and national park of dunes and wildlife, and the long, narrow peninsula of **Jandía**, with its celebrated beach resorts, in the south. Inland, volcanic mountain ranges dot the landscape, traversed by dried-up riverbeds, which have cut ravines through the wide regions of the *malpaís*, the cinder-strewn 'badlands'.

DON'T MISS

*** **National Underwater Park:** finest submarine park in the Canaries.
** **Valley of Palms:** oasis with ancient buildings.
** **Pájara Parish Church:** fine example of 16th-century architecture.
** **Jandía Mountain:** highest point on the island, magnificent views.
** **La Oliva:** 18th-century colonial buildings.
** **Dunes National Park:** mini-Sahara of undulating white sand dunes.

Opposite: *The windswept Jandía peninsula with 26km (16 miles) of glorious sandy beaches.*

FUERTEVENTURA

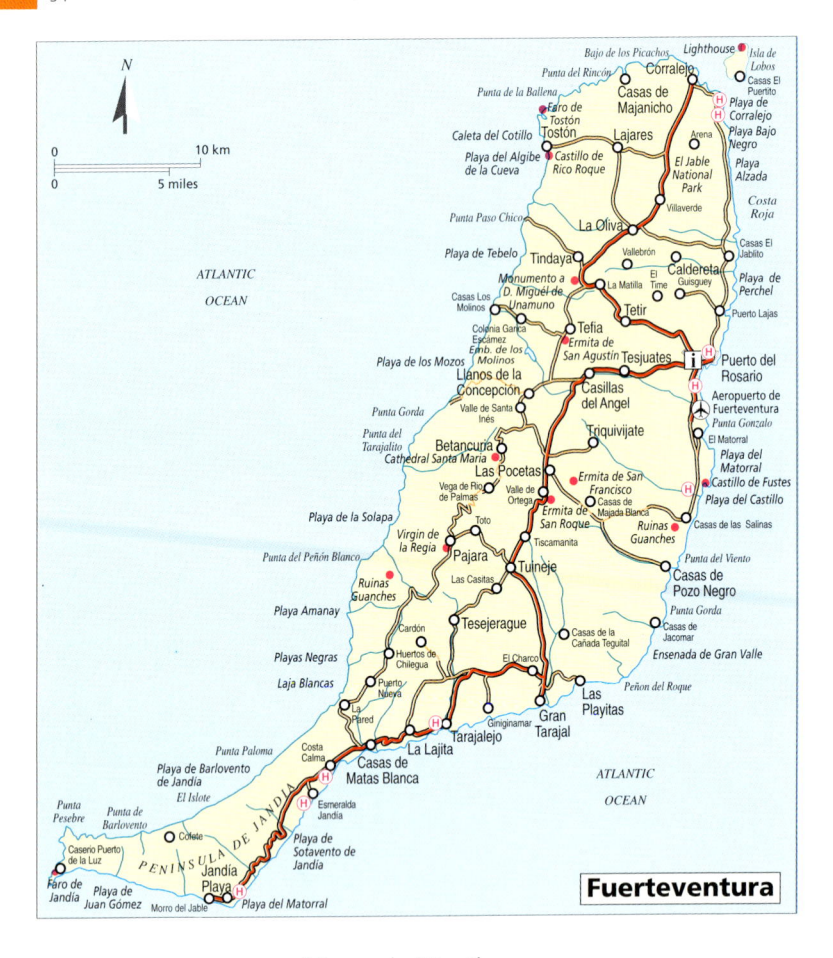

Man-made Attractions

Apart from the numerous natural attractions of Fuerteventura, the island also has a number of fascinating architectural monuments. Jean de Béthancourt, the first colonist, founded the **Santa María Cathedral** at Betancuria as early as the first years of the 15th century, but it was destroyed by pirates in 1539. The site, set in the wild interior, is dramatic. Later, Franciscan monks built several beautiful hermitages and churches throughout the island, notably at **El Time**, **La Olivia**, **Antigua**, and **Pájara**. Most are well preserved and immensely photogenic, as are the island's many windmills. Some of the mills are still operational. One is now a restaurant, and others lend their picturesque silhouettes to the barren skyline. Colonists left several ancient forts behind, reminders of the Canary Islands' violent history. **El Tostón** castle, at Costillo, is a fine example of the island's early fortifications. Civil architecture from the past includes the grandiose **Casa de los Coroneles** at La Olivia, which dates back to the 18th century.

Puerto del Rosario

The capital city of Fuerteventura has changed location several times over the past century or so. In 1836, the town of **Betancuria** took over the mantle of capital from **Antigua**, and, in 1860, the town of **Puerto de Cabras**, (Port of Goats), founded in 1797, became the island's administrative centre. In 1957, for a variety of reasons, the name of Cabras was changed to Puerto del Rosario (Port of the Rosary). The city is located on a natural bay on the eastern side of the island. The long harbour arm and portside installations were built as early as 1837. Today, the port supports a large fishing fleet and is home to the inter-island ferries.

THE FOREIGN LEGION

The advent of the Spanish Foreign Legion has been a more recent thorn in the Fuerteventuran side.

Relinquishing its hold on the Spanish Sahara, the Foreign Legion shifted its base to the island in 1975. An estimated force of 10,000 men almost doubled the island's population. Today, entrenched in Puerto del Rosario's barracks, the army has cordoned off several sites on Fuerteventura for military exercises.

Below: *Military statues reflect past glories in the gardens of the Spanish Foreign Legion's barracks.*

Around the Town

The population of Puerto del Rosario is around 8500, excluding the Foreign Legion. The seat of Government is located here, as are the headquarters and barracks of the **Foreign Legion**. Below the Legionnaire's office, in beautiful, terraced gardens, there is a celebration of the exploits of the Legion in an interesting collection of statues, momentoes, memorials and weaponry.

FUERTEVENTURA

Puerto del Rosario is said to be the brain-child of a past mayor, who dictated that no building in the city should exceed a certain height, and even now only one skyscraper dominates the skyline. Although there aren't really old buildings here, the old part of the town, with its narrow cobbled streets and restful squares, is certainly worth exploring, as are the craft shops like **Artesania**.

Playa Blanca *

Many of the visitors avoid Rosario and head for the beaches, or the older and more interesting towns and sites on the island. In the first week of October, Puerto del Rosario holds its annual festival, the **Fiesta de la Virgen de Rosario**. Just south of the city is a beautiful beach, Playa Blanca, which is overlooked by the **National Parador**. Another kilometre further south is the island's only airport which lies between the coastal road and the sea.

NORTH FROM PUERTO DEL ROSARIO

The main road north, towards La Olivia, passes the old airport and Devil's Claw mountain before a track leads off to the left towards the **Las Mercedes Hermitage** at El Time village. Further along the main road, just before La Oliva Plain, there is a monument to the well-known exiled writer Miguel de Unamuno on **Montaña Quemada** or Burnt Mountain.

The fascinating town of **La Oliva** boasts the interesting 18th-century military residence **Casa de los Coroneles**, the Aztec-style fronted **Casa del Capellan**, and the 18th-century **Nuestra Señora de Candelaria**.

HOW DID FUERTEVENTURA GET ITS NAME?

Fuerteventura in ancient times was a lush, fertile island known as **Herbania**. Ecological disasters make this name inappropriate today. Conquistadore Jean de Béthancourt is supposed to have said 'Que fuerte ventura!' (what a great adventure) when he first landed. The name might be a corruption of *el viento fuerte* – the name for the strong wind which blows almost constantly.

NORTH FROM PUERTO DEL ROSARIO

Dramatic in its lonely surroundings, the Casa de los Coroneles dates from the 18th- century and was the residence of the military commanders of the island up until the end of the 19th century. The coat of arms over its entrance gate is surmounted by a cross and is indicative of Spain's Catholic influence. Its balconies are also typical of Canarian workmanship. Towers at each end of the façade give the building a fortified look.

Past La Oliva, a road west leads to **El Cotillo**, the 15th-century site of **Maxorata**, seat of **King Guixe** of the Guanches. Cotilla is a small fishing village and there are some lovely beaches nearby.

Heading towards **Puerto del Tostón** you will come across the well-known resort of **Caleta Fueste** and the tiny fishing port which is overlooked by the fascinating antique **Rico Roque** tower.

On the road towards **Corralejo**, take time to scale **Bayuyo Peak** for breathtaking scenic views. An easy climb to the summit affords vistas across volcanic cinders and sand dunes to the **Isle of Lobos** to the north, and the peak of **Caldera Hondo** (272m; 870ft) to the south.

> **LOCAL CUSTOMS**
>
> Like many European countries with a hot climate, the tradition of the *siesta* continues on most of the islands. Between 13:00 and 16:00 towns and villages will be eerily deserted, so this isn't a good time to go sightseeing or shopping. Locals will be enjoying a long lunch and a short nap, so why not do the same? The *paseo* (promenade) is the early evening stroll where families parade in their finery before going off to eat at 20:00.

Below: *The busy ferry terminal and popular resort of Corralejo.*

> **NUDE SUNBATHING**
>
> Since the Canaries continue to be part of Spain, which is still a very Catholic country, visitors in search of an all-over tan will find that nude sunbathing is still generally frowned upon. In the large resorts there are designated nudist beaches, and topless sunbathing is commonplace. Nudists congregate in the sand dunes at **Maspalomas** on Gran Canaria and at **Corralejo** on Fuerteventura.

Above: *Corralejo's sparsely vegetated sand dunes, now a national park and habitat for rare birds.*

> **DESERT WILDLIFE**
>
> In the north of the island, Dunes National Park preserves some of the rarer indigenous creatures, particularly birds. Forty different birds breed on the island, including the ubiquitous canary. The ruff, snipe, curlew, hoopoe, sand grouse and rare Fuerteventura houbara, bustard and Fuerteventuran chat, attract birdwatchers to the park. In the south, the mountain terrain is home to the osprey, Canarian buzzard, Egyptian vulture, quail and partridge. The coast is prolific with birdlife such as waders, oystercatchers, razorbills, gannet and the occasional flock of flamingo and spoonbill. It is here that a fossil ostrich egg was once found.

Corralejo **

This popular resort is situated on the northern tip of the island. The fishing port is flanked by rolling dunes giving way to fabulous sandy resort beaches. Corralejo is known throughout the Canary islands for its beaches, but its centre has been a little spoilt by modernization. Local fishermen, however, still congregate in bars by the quayside, and their gaily painted craft add colour to the small port. From here you can hop onto the ferry across **El Rio** to the nearby islet of **Lobos** (Wolf Island, named for its seals, or sea-wolves), or to the distant island of **Lanzarote**.

Both of the region's wonderful beaches, **Playa de Corralejo** and **Playa del Moro**, lie to the east of the town.

Dunes National Park **

The road east from the outskirts of the town passes the Corralejo Beach Hotel complex and follows the edge of the Dunes National Park as it hugs the coastline back to Puerto del Rosario. The park – a vast desert – is also a nature reserve for several species of rare birds, some of which breed here. Where there is any vegetation, mostly in the gullies and dry gorges to the edge of the sandy desert, the North African ground squirrel will be found among sparse glasswort, sea spurge and tamarisk.

Playa del Perchel *

As the road nears the city, the scenery gives way to small volcanic mountains and lava outcrops. Halfway along the coast between Morro beach and the city is the popular beach of Playa del Perchel.

WEST FROM PUERTO ROSARIO

If you take the coast road south from Puerto del Rosario you will pass the beach resort of **Castillo de Fustes** on the left, which was built around a 1740 watchtower. After this is the **Casa de las Salinas** (the old Salt House) which overlooks the early salt pans. After passing a number of ancient Guanche ruins on the left, follow the route to the old capital, Antigua. The old **Hermitage of San Francisco** is on the right. It roughly marks the centre of the island, which you will pass before reaching the 18th-century town of **Antigua**, situated on a parched plain and breaking the rugged skyline. This was once the island's capital and its charming whitewashed houses are a mixture of Moorish and Spanish architectural styles. The area around the town is famous for its many windmills. Stop for a meal at the 200-year-old **El Molino** round restaurant just outside the town and make a point of seeing the beautifully restored granary with its wooden ceiling.

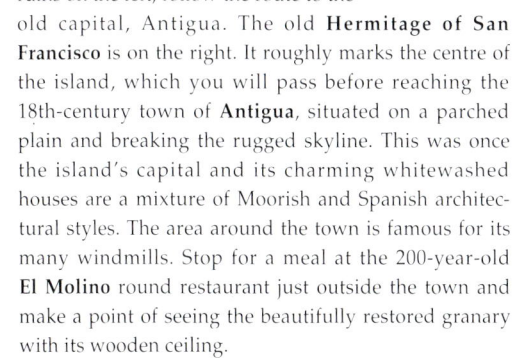

Betancuria **

In a magnificent mountain setting, Betancuria was named after the 15th-century Norman conqueror, Jean de Béthancourt, who built a fort as refuge from pirate

MIGUEL DE UNAMUNO

Fuerteventura was used over the centuries as a place of exile for those who criticized the Spanish government. The writer and philosopher Miguel de Unamuno (1854–1936), however, seems to have rather enjoyed his brief exile here in 1924. Calling the island an 'oasis in the desert of civilization', 'a naked, arid, barren, bone-hard land which soothes the spirit', he obviously appreciated the solitude.

Above: *El Castillo (also known as Caleta de Fuste), a beach resort built around an 18th-century watch tower.*
Left: *Betancuria, a lovely old colonial town named after a 15th-century conquistador, Jean de Béthancourt, and once the island's capital.*

Cinder Cultivation

Fuerteventura is the driest of the Canary's seven islands. Less than 15cm (6in) of water falls here anually. The volcanic soil is rich. Apart from a few precious springs in the south, and some wells which produce brackish water, irrigation on the island has been the product of man's ingenuity. A certain type of volcanic cinder, mined in the north, was found to have properties which retain night mists and dews. By spreading this mineral on small stone-walled plots of land, terraced into the hillside, the islanders have been able to raise crops of cereals and vegetables. With the aqueous stratas increasingly eluding the reach of windmill bores, cistern ships supply the island with water from the mainland.

attacks. It is now a national monument and contains some interesting relics. Besides this monument there is also the **Museo Arqueológico,** housing artefacts dating back to Guanche times. Betancuria's church of **Santa María** is an architectural gem. The ceiling has wonderful decorated beams and the gilded high altar dates back to the 17th century.

Once the most important town in the Canary island group, Betancuria was incorporated into Spain's Crown of Castile in 1405, and its cathedral, **Iglesia Santa María de Betancuria**, formed the seat of the Lords of Fuerteventura. Béthancourt's standard can still be seen in the cathedral church, and the island's longest ruling families, the Saavedras, had their coat of arms engraved on the exterior of the church. This was once the island's cathedral until it was destroyed by pirates in 1539.

Valley of Palms **

The Valley of Palms, or the **Vega del Rio de Palmas**, lies in the shadow of the Hermitage and Sanctuary of the Virgen de Peña, Fuerteventura's patron saint. For absolute tranquillity and shade, this little oasis, which is dominated by the peak of **Gran Montana**, is unsurpassed on the island.

Iglesia de la Virgen de la Regla **

A short way south is the small, pretty village of **Pájara**, or 'Tiny Hen'. Dominating the square is a lovely church, the **Iglesia de la Virgen de la Regla**, which dates back to 1645. It has a charming interior with beautifully painted altar screens in a simple floral design. The church portal, which is believed to date from the 16th century, is executed in pink sandstone and carved with symbols of suns, snakes, lions and doves.

Below: *Animals are practical farming aids on Fuerteventura's terraced farms.*

Milling around Windmills

Heading east from Pájara, you'll find the village of **Tuineje**, with its many windmills which are well worth visiting. Windmills were used to grind the grain used for **gofio**, once the island's staple food. **Tiscamanita** has a well-preserved, three-storey windmill. A similar one with six sails can be viewed at **Llanos de la Concepcíon** and there are several at **Villaverde**. There are interesting mills at **Lajares**, **El Cotillo** and **Carralejo**. A few have lost their outbuildings because the stone blocks have been used for houses or walls. Some are in working order but many need to be renovated. Lime kilns are often mistaken for windmill ruins, owing to the state of disrepair of many mills. You may find it difficult to distinguish which is which from a distance.

Above: *Windmills in the interior make practical use of the strong winds that blow across the island.*

SOUTH FROM PUERTO DEL ROSARIO

In order to reach the **Jandía Peninsula** which has more than half of the island's beaches, take the coastal road from Puerto del Rosario. This road passes the island's second port, **Gran Tarajal**. The peaks of the Jandía Peninsula here are just high enough to catch a little rain from the prevailing trade winds, sufficient to raise exportable quantities of tomatoes, shipped from this port. The road also passes the seaside resorts of **Tarajalejo** and **Playa Puerto Rico**. The longer, inland route is far more scenic. On your way back to Pájara, and then to **La Pared** village, you will notice that the scenery begins to change dramatically. Jagged gorges and volcanic cones become even more rugged as the road winds through one of the island's most isolated regions.

Passing through **Pájara**, historians will look in vain for traces of the mini-Hadrian's Wall which used to divide the twin kingdoms of the island in Guanche days. As you

---

THE VERDINO

The Fuerteventuran dog, the Verdino, named for its generally greenish hue, is a special breed of dog which has been indigenous to the Canary Islands for over 2000 years. It is thought that the name for the islands itself comes from the Roman word for dog – *canis*. The ancient breed has survived in its purest form on Fuerteventura and is used as a guard dog for herds of sheep and goats. In the early 16th century, this lithe, gracious hound was so feared by the conquistadores that they were condemned to death. Each Fuerteventuran shepherd was permitted to own one hound, provided it was controlled by a boy at all times.

Right: *Strong Atlantic breezes make the Jandía Peninsula a windsurfer's paradise.*
Below: *Exotic fish swim in abundance in the azure ocean waters.*
Opposite: *Eye-catching replica of an old-fashioned boat, half-buried in the southern sands.*

TOP TRIPS

Although Fuerteventura appears barren and of little interest on the face of it, there are numerous trips which reveal its hidden secrets. From **Corralejo** you could hop on a boat to **Wolf Island** or do a day trip to **Lanzarote**, or take a taxi tour around Fuerteventura. Big game fisherman can go on a six-hour shark fishing trip from the **Jandía Hotel**.

cross the ancient boundary between the kingdoms of Maxorata in the north, and that of Jandía in the south, the island's nickname of 'Solitude Isle' bites home. Entering the 'bottle neck' or isthmus of the Jandía Península, the road after Pared turns east from the **Barlovento** (leeward) coast, and the Club Aldiana resort, towards the **Sotavento** (windward) beaches.

The desolate landscape on the way to Morro suddenly materializes into the spectacular vista of turquoise seas and the built-up resort area of **Matas Blancas** to the left. This is the well-known 25km (15 mile) beach lying to the north of the Sotavento coast. From here, picture-postcard beaches are fronted by tourist developments like the **Canada del Rio**, the **Costa Calma**, **Playa Esmeralda Jandía** and the vast sprawl of **Los Goriones**. The road takes you to the port town of **Morro del Jable** and steep cliffs start to line the beautiful coastline. This is an important commercial fishing port and its restaurants certainly confirm its commitment to maintaining the tradition of seafood menus. You will see crescents of sandy beaches on the left side of the road, while saw-toothed volcanic mountains provide a dramatic backdrop to the right. Smaller resorts include **Playa Juan Gomez** beaches and the villages of **Casa de Joros** and **Casa Cueva de la Negra**. The dominant shoreline feature is the **Playa de las Pillas**, a long stretch of beach running east to west along the southernmost point of the island.

SOUTH FROM PUERTO DEL ROSARIO

Jandía Mountain **

As you head towards the tip of the island, the mountain, which rises like a pyramid inland is the 807m (2647ft) Jandía Mountain. This is Fuerteventura's highest point. The rocks here are some of the oldest in the entire Canarian archipelago.

Caserio Puerto de la Luz **

Near the southernmost tip of Fuerteventura is the lighthouse at Caserio Puerto de la Luz. This area, and the majority of the peninsula, was given to German engineer (and Nazi sympathizer) Gustave Winter by President Franco, for services rendered. Rumoured to have been in league with the Germans during World War II, Winter was later suspected of harbouring war criminals fleeing to South America. This region, and the Sotavento coastline, is a favourite holiday resort with German tourists. The coast is now a **national underwater park**.

The west coast, consisting of 20km (12½ miles) of white sandy beach and lying a couple of kilometres from the the giant resorts of the Sotavento coast, is virtually deserted, principally because it is difficult to get to. The Atlantic breezes have created some really magnificent beaches, such as the **Playa de Barlovento de Jandía** and the **Playa de Cofete**, which is quite near to an ancient abandoned hamlet. On this side of the peninsula the winds have carved weird and fantastic natural sculptures from the volcanic and sandstone cliffs which guard the shoreline.

WINDSURFING

Windsurfing is an enormously popular sport in the Canaries and the **Jandía peninsula** in particular attracts surfers from all over the world. In August, an annual world windsurfing championships are held at **Playa de Sotavento** which is a very wide, flat beach.

Fuerteventura at a Glance

BEST TIMES TO VISIT
Fuerteventura has almost a North African climate: little variation in temperature year-round. Winter nights are cool, and a jacket is recommended.

GETTING THERE
Most visitors, except those from the Spanish mainland, arrive by air at **Los Estancas International Airport**, south of the capital. There are **ferry services** from Cádiz for passengers and cars to the island.

GETTING AROUND
The best way to get around is to hire a **car** and select where you want to go. You will need an international driving licence. Drive on the right. Seat belts are compulsory. Speed limits vary from 60kph (35mph) in built up areas, to 120kph (75mph) on motorways. Many petrol stations close on Sundays and few take credit cards. There is a **bus service**, but timetables are erratic. Travel agents can advise of bus times, and also organize a day's **taxi** tour of the island: a set package including lunch. Long-distance taxi rides have a set rate and short distances are metered.

WHERE TO STAY

Puerto del Rosario
LUXURY
Parador National de Fuerteventura, Playa Blanca; tel: (928) 85 11 50, fax: 85 11 58; near town, homely, in traditional Canarian setting.

BUDGET
Roquemar, Ruperto Gonzales Negrin 1; tel: (928) 85 03 59; basic facilities, central location.
Hotel Tamasite, Calle Léon y Castillo 9; tel: (928) 85 02 80; basic facilities, convenient.

Corralejo
LUXURY
Dunapark, General Franco, s/n; tel: (928) 53 52 51, fax: 53 54 91; central, excellent facilities, access for handicapped.

MID-RANGE
Apartamentos Corralejo Beach, Ave General Franco; tel: (928) 86 63 15, fax 86 63 17; excellent facilites.
Riu Palace Tres Islas, Playa de Corralejo; tel: (928) 53 57 00, fax (928) 53 58 58; on the beach, all rooms have terraces.

BUDGET
Corralejo Hotel, Calle Colon 12, Playa Corralejo; tel: (928) 53 52 46; basic, on the beach.
Riu Oliva Beach, Playa de Corralejo; tel: (928) 86 61 00; fax: (928) 86 61 54; Olympic-size pool, views of beach and sand dune park.

Jandia
LUXURY
Princesa Star, Avda. del Saladar, 28, Jandia-Pajara; tel: (928) 54 04 30, fax: 54 02 18; top hotel here, with all facilites.
Hotel Riu Calypso, Carr. General de Morro Jable; tel: (928) 54 00 26, fax: 54 07 30; excellent facilities, pool.

MID-RANGE
Apartamentos Atlantica, Avda. del Saladar 28, Jandia-Pajara; tel: (928) 87 60 17; good location with facilities.
Los Gorriones, Playa la Barca; tel: (928) 87 08 50; Jandia's first hotel with three pools.

BUDGET
Fiesta Casa Atlantica, Jandia Playa; tel: (928) 87 60 17; reasonable facilities, with all the basic requirements.

Canada del Rio (Pájara)
LUXURY
Riu Fuerteventura, Playa Urbanizacion Canada del Rio; tel: (928) 54 73 44; fax: 54 70 97; new four-star installation.
Sol Elite Gorriones, Playa Barca, s/n; tel: (928) 54 70 25, fax: 54 70 00; magnificent location with all facilities including pool and golf course.

MID-RANGE
Taro Beach, Urbanizacion Canada del Rio, Costa Calma-Pajara; tel: (928) 54 70 98, fax: 50 70 76; an excellent range of facilities but quite expensive.
Club Solyventura, tel: (928) 87 03 32, fax: 54 70 00; has a range of facilites, including a good swimming pool.

Antigua
MID-RANGE
Apartments El Castillo, Urbanizacion Castillo Caleta de Fustes; tel: (928) 87 81 00; beautifully located, chalet-type accommodation.

Fuerteventura at a Glance

La Oliva
MID-RANGE
Apartments Los Barqueros, Avenida Grandes Playas, s/n; tel: (928) 86 60 72; well-serviced apartments.
Hotel Hopalco, Avenida General Franco 45; tel: (928) 86 60 40; has very good accommodation.

WHERE TO EAT

Corralejo
La Barca, Calle Generalisimo Franco; tel: (928) 86 60 54; tasty seafood dishes.
Casa de Candelaria, Calle Almirante Carrero Blanco; tel: (928) 86 60 97; international cuisine.
Chato y Manuela, Calle Isaac Peral; tel: (928) 86 62 86; excellent local dishes.
La Taberna, Calle H. Cortez 3; tel: (928) 53 50 27; typical traditional fare.

Jandía
La Andaluza, Playa del Matorral; tel: (928) 87 60 47; great seafood selection.
Casa Juan, tel: (928) 87 63 60; local dishes, traditional.
El Meson, Playa Paradiso; tel: (928) 54 02 03; range of dishes.
Taberna del Pescador, Playa del Matorral; tel: (928) 87 64 11; Famous fish dishes.

Antigua
Casa Frasquita, Caleta de Fustes; good local fare.
Molino Antigua, tel: (928) 87 82 20; interesting mill location, good traditional fare.

La Oliva
Mariquito Hierro, Calle Maria Hierro; tel: (928) 86 80 49 specializes in traditional food.

TOURS AND EXCURSIONS

Although Fuerteventura appears barren and of little interest on the face of it, there are numerous trips which reveal its hidden secrets.
Northern Tour of the Island: Ultramar Express, Hotel Rui Oliva Beach, La Oliva, tel: (928) 86 62 51; or Viajes Canyrama, Carretera Carrero Blanco, tel: (928) 86 62 25.
Western or Southern Round Tour: Viajes Insular, Avenida 1 de Mayo 52, Puerto del Rosario, tel: (928) 85 05 94; or Viajes Paukner, Avenida Generalisimo, 34, La Oliva, tel: (928) 86 60 10.
Lobos Island: visit from Corralejo, taking one of the day tours to Lanzarote, also from Corralejo; Ultramar Express, Hotel Rui Oliva Beach, La Oliva, tel: (928) 86 62 51.
Taxi tour of the island from Corralejo: Autos Estupinan, Avenida Gernalisimo 18, Corralijo, tel: (928) 86 60 48.
Shark and deep-sea fishing trips: Escualo, Corralejo; tel: (928) 85 13 29 or Pez Verlero, Corralejo, tel: (928) 86 61 73.
Round trip (windmills): Viajes Elba, Carretera Princesa Tamonante, Gran Tarajal, Tuineji, tel: (928) 87 00 33.

USEFUL CONTACTS

Corralejo: Barakuda Club, Diving Centre, tel: (928) 86 62 43.
Jandia: Aldiana Club, tel: (928) 54 14 47.
Antigua: El Castillo-Caleta de Fustes, tel: (928) 87 81 00/1.
Deep-sea Fishing: Escualo, tel: (928) 85 13 29.
Pez Velero, tel: (928) 86 61 73.
Tourist Information Centre, Avda 1 de Mayo 33, Puerto del Rosario, tel/: (928) 85 10 24.
Cabildo Insular, Carretera 1 de Mayo 39, Puerto del Rosario, tel: (928) 85 14 00.
Areopuerto Los Estancas Puerto del Rosario, tel: (928) 85 12 50.
IBERIA Airways 23 de Mayo 11, Puerto del Rosario, tel: (928) 85 08 02.
Transmediterranea Shipping, Léon y Castillo 46, Puerto del Rosario, tel: (928) 85 00 95.

FUERTEVENTURA	J	F	M	A	M	J	J	A	S	O	N	D
AVERAGE TEMP. °C	17	18	18	19	20	22	23	24	24	23	21	18
AVERAGE TEMP. °F	63	65	65	66	68	72	73	75	75	73	70	65
HOURS OF SUN DAILY	6	8	7	7	8	10	10	8	6	6	5	5
RAINFALL mm	36	8	2	11	2	0	0	0	6	3	58	9
RAINFALL in	1.5	0	0	0	0	0	0	0	0	0	2	0
DAYS OF RAINFALL	7	6	5	4	2	1	1	1	2	6	10	9

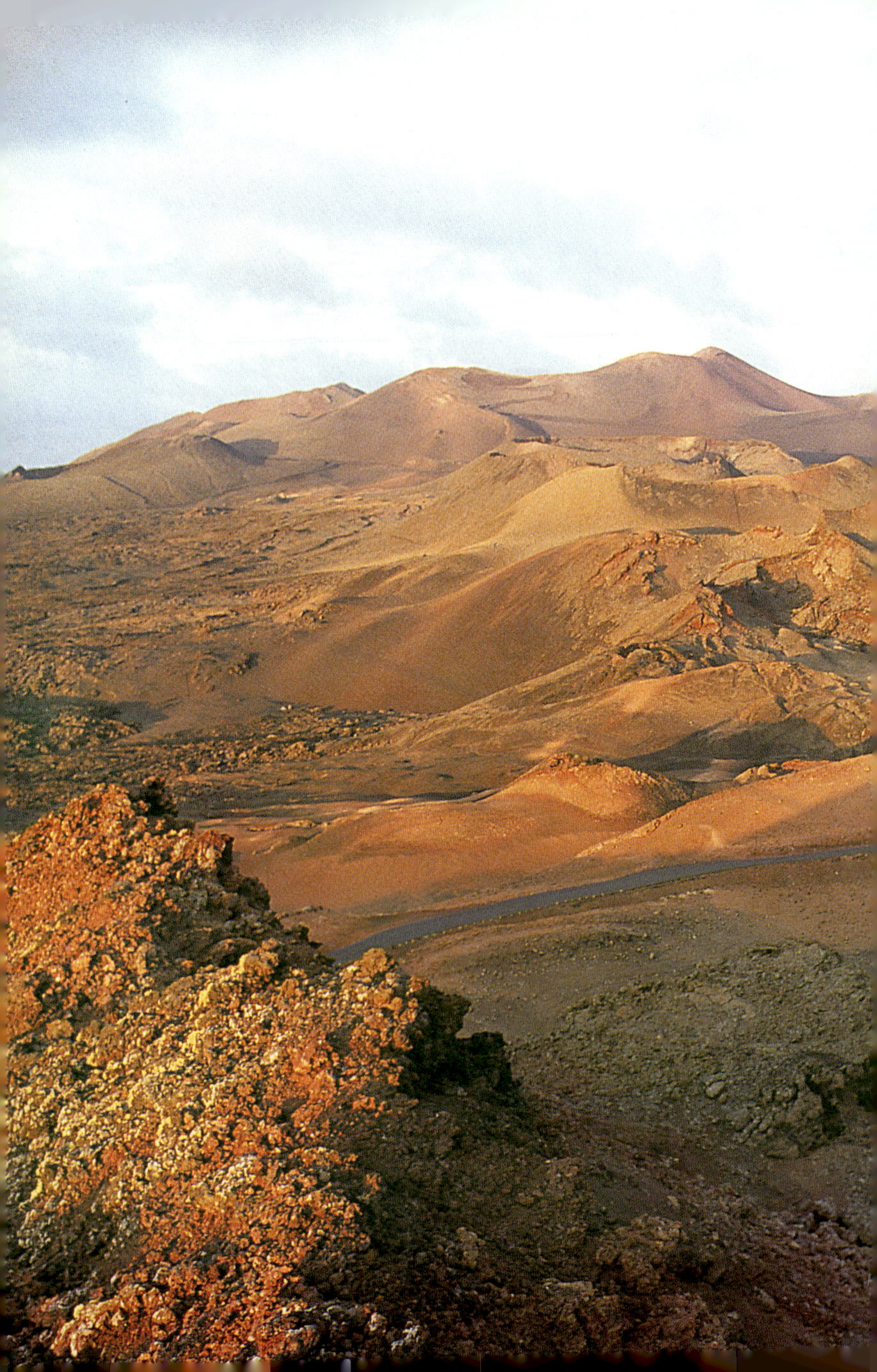

5
Lanzarote

Battered and scarred by the ravages of nature, Lanzarote is the Canaries' fourth largest island. There are over 300 volcanoes sprinkled throughout the island and in 1730 a six-year period of eruptions began, transforming the face of Lanzarote. A quarter of the island was blanketed with ash and the surface sculpted into the desolate, pock-marked landscape that exists today.

Lanzarote is a hauntingly beautiful island, unspoilt by rampant commercialism or insensitive development. The island is dotted with installations by artist César Manrique such as the **Mirador del Rio** and **Jameos del Agua** that imaginatively, yet sensitively, exploit the landscape without spoiling its charm. Islanders themselves are very environmentally aware and there are no high-rise concrete jungles to mar Lanzarote's natural beauty.

Surprisingly enough the land is fertile and prosperous, due to the *eneranado* water conservation method and cultivation of lava soil. Intricate arcs of rock and cinder terraces provide perfect conditions for growing vegetables, fruit and vines. **Malmsey wine** is an island speciality, a sweet yet sublime treat.

Today's tourists converge on **Timanfaya National Park** to explore the lava flows and experience the sheer force of nature. Fabulous beaches, picturesque villages and historic monuments all add to Lanzarote's charm. Off the island's northern tip is La Graciosa, a tranquil, rocky outcrop popular with fishermen and sun-worshippers.

Don't Miss

*** **Timanfaya National Park:** eerie lunar landscape.
*** **Jameos del Agua** and **Cueva Los Verdes:** fascinating volcanic caverns.
*** **Mirador del Rio:** glorious views over La Graciosa.
*** **El Golfo:** luminous green lagoon inside a broken volcano cone.
** **Santa Barbara Fort:** near Teguise, dating from the 14th century.

Opposite: *Sunset lights up the Mountains of Fire in the Timanfaya National Park, a volcanic wilderness.*

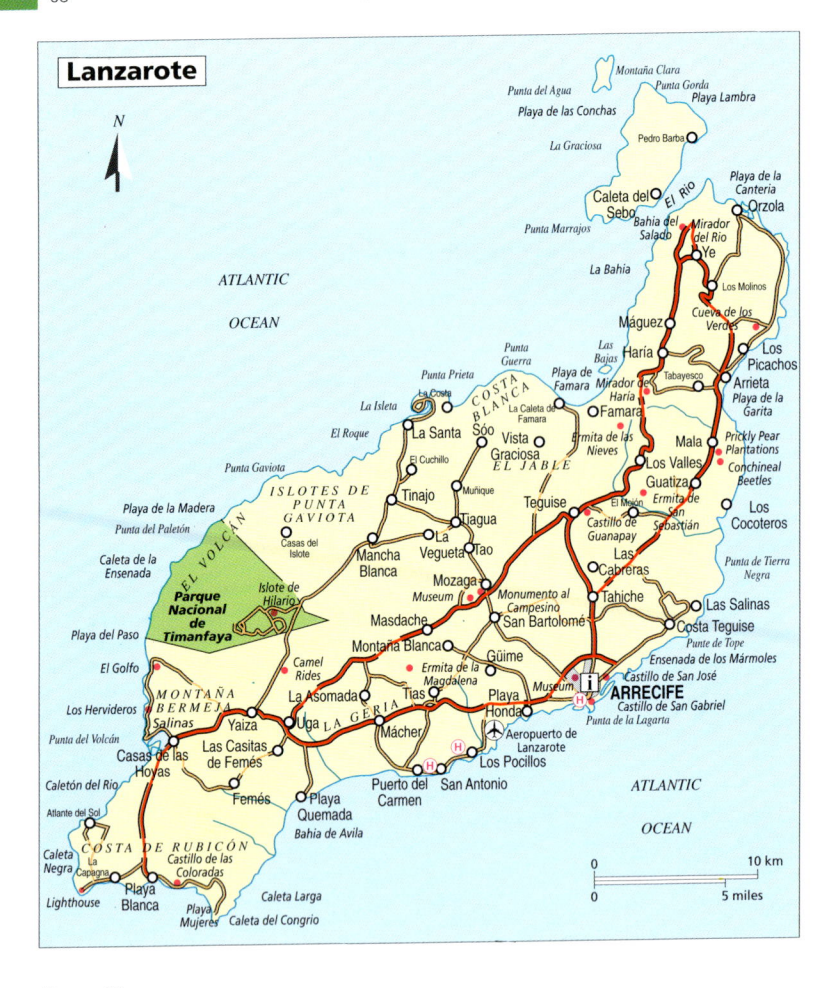

EARLY HISTORY

King Juba II of Mauretania, West Africa, visited the island in the 1st century AD and reports about the islands were circulated by **Pliny the Elder**, who called Lanzarote and Fuerteventura *purpurariae*, after the purple dye produced from the local *orchilla* lichen. The first attempt at settlement was made by Arab explorers who, after subduing the local inhabitants, built a fort in the centre of the island in the 10th century. Around 300 years later in 1312, the Genoese **Lanzarotto Malocello** led an expedition here, calling the island after himself, and claiming it for Portugal. Spain arrived in the form of

ARRECIFE

Fernando Peraza's troops, who sacked the island in 1385, only to be followed by the Norman invasion of **Gadafir de la Salle** and **Jean de Béthancourt** in 1402. The family of **Diego de Herrera** ruled Lanzarote for most of the 15th century and it was incorporated into the Spanish crown in 1479. The 16th and 17th centuries saw a succession of pirate attacks, and the population waxed and waned throughout the 19th century. Tourism proper on Lanzarote began in the 1970s and has since become the island's main foreign currency earner.

> **ISLAND HOPPING**
>
> Connections between most of the seven islands are generally good. Current timetables should be consulted as both flights and ferry sailings can vary. For those who wish to visit every island in the Canaries and see each island on the way, a good three weeks should be set aside. Most visitors who wish to see two or more islands generally base themselves on Lanzarote and concentrate on seeing the three eastern islands by taking the regular ferries. Although all the islands except La Gomera has an airport, it is cheaper, but more time-consuming, to take ferries or jet-foils between the islands.

ARRECIFE

Lanzarote's capital, Arrecife, is located about halfway along the east coast, facing south. Its name comes from the reefs and islets which are dotted throughout the wide bay. This is the closest port of the Canary Islands to the Saharan coast of Africa, and its fishing fleet benefits from the mainland's prolific fishing grounds. Until about 200 years ago, Teguise was the capital of Lanzarote. Consequently, Arrecife, in those days little more than a quiet coastal fishing port, has few of the historic attractions of the original capital.

Above: *Umbrellas and sunloungers line the beach at Puerto del Carmen, Lanzarote's most popular resort.*
Below: *Ancient cannon guard the fortress walls of San Gabriel in Arrecife.*

Fort of San Gabriel ★★
The two prominent sites of this rather bland capital are the forts of **San Gabriel** and **San José**, standing at either side of the arm of the bustling harbour. Designed by

Right: *César Manrique's 1968 museum and rural restaurant is located in the geographical centre of Lanzarote.*

> **MOST FAMOUS SON**
>
> Lanzarote's most famous citizen was the architect, painter and sculptor **César Manrique** (1920–1992). He wanted to protect his island from over-development and thought that architecture made from natural materials should exist in harmony with the environment. It's largely thanks to him that Lanzarote has been spared the horrors of high-rises and garish advertising.

the island's first prison governor, Don Gaspar de Salcedo, in 1573, the Fortress of San Gabriel was burnt down in an attack on the natural harbour in 1586. The Italian engineer and architect to Felipe II, Leonardo Torriani, rebuilt the fort and reclad its four diamond-shaped corners in 1590. Today, the castle houses a small **Archaeological Museum**. A drawbridge, the **Puente de las Bolas**, links the El Quemado promontory on which the fort stands with the centre of the town. Open 9:00–13:00 and 15:00–18:00 daily.

Fort of San José ★★★

Standing between the Los Marmoles breakwater and El Puerto del Naos, to the north of the town, the 1799 Castillo de San José, built during Carlos III's reign, contains the **Museum of Contemporary Art**, with works by modern masters Picasso, Miró and the celebrated local artist, César Manrique. Above the dungeon art galley there is a good restaurant and bar.

Manrique's gallery is on Calle José Béthencourt and is one of the artist's famous murals. It is made from local lava and decorates the foyer of the old Gran Hotel, which still dominates Arrecife's harbourside skyline.

The town's pretty Municipal Park is also the work of César Manrique, and well worth a visit. The main church in the town is **San Gines** and the patron saint's day is on 25 August, an exuberant fiesta with fireworks, music and a camel parade.

Arrecife has three beaches: **Playa Blanca**, **El Reducto** and **Guacineta**. The only commercial airport on the island is about 6km (4 miles) south of Arrecife town, past the resort of **Playa Honda**. Playa El Reducto, situated just south of Arrecife, is the town's best beach.

TIMANFAYA NATIONAL PARK

It takes about three hours to do a complete tour of Timanfaya Park, an atmospheric volcanic wilderness created during the 18th-century eruptions. A visit to the park must be done through the organized tourist routes as it is forbidden to enter the area unaccompanied. Approach the **Montañas del Fuego** (Mountains of Fire) of the volcanic area of Timanfaya by way of the picturesque village of **Yaiza**. The entrance to the park is signposted with the National Park emblem of a devil waving a pitchfork. One of the best ways of exploring the park is on a camel and there are regular excursions which leave from Uga village. It pays to bear in mind that camels are rather uncomfortable, noisy, smelly beasts with unbelievably bad breath!

PLAYING WITH FIRE

Lanzarote is famed for its novel, natural ovens. The area is known as the Timanfaya, and the cooking site is in the **Montañas del Fuego**, or Mountains of Fire. A few centimetres below ground, the volcanic activity can range from 100° to over 400°C (752°F) on the hillock of **Tinecheide**. Potatoes can be baked in the soil here, and local guides demonstrate the various wonders of the fearful land which bubbles in molten frenzy just a short distance under the visitor's feet. The mountain of Timanfaya, which gave its name to the area, is an extinct volcanic cone which rises to 510m (1673ft) and can be reached by camels which are provided locally.

Below: *Camel treks are a novel way of exploring Timanfaya's lava flows.*

> **SALT OF THE SEA**
>
> Salt, an important commodity, especially in the early days when meat had to be preserved, became a major industry in Lanzarote when the economy dwindled during the mid-19th century. Today, three major salt pan areas still produce salt at **Janubio**, the **Salinas del Rio**, and north of Arrecife. The large works at **El Charco** has now been developed for tourism. More than 10,000 tonnes are extracted from sea water each year and are used to salt down fish. The salt pans of the Salinas del Rio are pink, attributed to the minute salt water shrimps which attract flocks of flamingo. Lanzarote is the only Canary island to produce salt, although the salt houses at the **Salinas del Carmen**, on Fuerteventura, stand testament to its past industry.

Below: *Malpais, or badlands territory in Timanfaya.*

Near the Islote de Hilario parking lot, named after a hermit who lived alone on this spot for 50 years with just a donkey as company, is the **El Diablo** (Devil) Restaurant. This interesting building was designed in glass and lava by César Manrique. Meals in the restaurant are cooked over the natural volcanic heat. The temperature, just below the surface, is demonstrated outside the restaurant by guides who conduct various experiments showing how brushwood fed into a hole instantly bursts into flame, and water is turned into an explosion of steam.

Take the opportunity to go on the spectacular hourly **Lunar Ride** by coach up into the multi-coloured volcanic *malpaís* (badlands) to look into smoking craters and for views across the desert-like moonscape to the distant farms and the sea. Unfortunately, it is forbidden to take samples of volcanic rock from the park.

THE SOUTHERN ROUTE

Some visitors prefer to see the volcanic region at sunset, because of the fantastic colours produced by the rays of the sinking sun. Whether taking the morning or evening tour it's well worthwhile combining your visit to the Timanfaya Park with a trip around the south of the island. Out of **Puerto del Carmen**, the road runs through the **La Geria** wine-producing region. It then passes through **Uga** village, reconstructed 10m (33ft) above the original village, which was buried in the volcanic eruptions of 1730. The flat roofs of the whitewashed houses here are designed to catch precious rainwater. See the sloping-sided little church of **San Isidro Labrador** and the exhibitions of Canarian wrestling at the Timanfaya Restaurant. The next town on the route to the west coast is **Yaiza**, said to be the most typical of all settlements on Lanzarote. The village square and 18th-century church of **Los Remedios** are extremely photogenic, as are the **Jardínes de la Era**.

Take the road south, towards the salt pans. A side road branches off to the beautiful bay of **El Golfo**, nestling in the half-moon remnants of a volcanic crater. The Salinas de Janubio, the desalination plant, is one of Lanzarote's trademarks and produces around 10,000 tonnes of salt a year which is used for preserving fish. The process of evaporation takes about four weeks. Vast checkerboard patterns of the flat salt pans are dotted with little pyramids of sea salt.

An irridescent turquoise lagoon beyond the salt pans is a haven for a variety of birds. The main road now runs south, to the beach resort of **Playa Blanca**. This was once a small fishing village but is now a thriving resort giving access to more beaches at **Papagayo**. The ferry to and from Puerto del Rosario and Fuerteventura runs from Playa Blanca.

A CENTRAL ROUTE

For six years after a tremendous volcanic eruption and earthquake ripped the heart out of Lanzarote in 1730, lava flows and ash and cinder fallout blanketed the land. A four-hour central island walk of around 13km (8 miles) will give you an insight into the extent of the holocaust. Starting off from **Uga**, at the heart of the **La Geria** wine region, after taking the Playa Blanca bus from Puerto del

Above: *The ferry to Fuerteventura leaves from the fast-growing resort of Playa Blanca.*

A LIMPID, LANGUID LAGOON

On the southwest coast of Lanzarote the visitor follows contorted lava which flows down to a spectacular, crescent-shaped lagoon. **El Golfo** lies in the remains of a half-eroded volcanic cone, forming a semi-circular amphitheatre around a vast pool. The inside of the crater has been terraced by wind and sea, and the noise of the nearby surf echoes around the natural auditorium. A unique mollusc, the clico, lives in the salt water of El Golfo. Salt is an important part of the economy here, as the huge salt pans of nearby **Janubio** show.

CULTIVATING CLOUDS

Few clouds break over this desert land but the ingenious islanders have developed a method of harvesting the moisture-laden trade winds. After the devastation of the 1730–36 volcanic eruptions, it looked as though Lanzarote would remain barren. Farmers, however, invented a unique system of man-made craters, surrounded by lava rock walls which, at night, trap the moisture in the air to feed the plants, vegetables, figs and vines which are planted in the 2.5m (8ft) diameter hollows. The low stone walls also protect the plants, creating a unique landscape. It looks as though the vines that produce the island's excellent Malmsey wine grow straight out of the black sand soil.

Carmen, walk through the village past the Timanfaya Restaurant and turn left at the sign 'Teguise por la Geria'. Uga is also the base for the Timanfaya camel tours. Pass two houses before turning right up the next track and look for a yellow-topped marker post. Continue right with **Mount Guardilama** in front, through vineyards enclosed by numerous hand-built stone walls. Take a left turn at the summit of the pass, where the vineyards come to an end. Take a short hike to the top of the slippery cindered Mount Guardilama for panoramic views over a blackened landscape. The land is pock-marked with crescent-shaped sheltering walls with a background of hazy volcanic cones, as well as the far arc of a white-fringed coastline. Head down along the main track keeping **La Asomada** village to the left, turning a short distance after the white building to the right.

Take a left turn at **Caminos los Olivos** and right at **Camino la Calderina** to the GC720 main road. Pass **Macher** village windmill, turning to the right and take a dirt track towards the sea. This passes Casa Romerito and if you turn left at Camino del Puerto it'll take you to the road leading back to **Puerto del Carmen**.

Left: *Musicians performing at Teguise play the timple, a small instrument similar to a ukelele.*
Opposite: *The crescent-shaped terraces of La Geria, Lanzarote's wine-growing region, are known as 'zocos'.*

TEGUISE

Often known as 'La Villa', this was the original capital of the island, a title transferred in 1852 to the port of Arrecife. Teguise is the first European town in the Canaries, and was founded by Maciot de Béthancourt, the nephew of the conquistador Jean de Béthancourt. Maciot married the daughter of Guadarfia, the last native king of the island. Teguise is named after the Guanche princess and dates back to the 10th century. The town was set back from the coast in order to avoid attacks by marauding pirates.

Santa Barbara Fort *

Although it used to be called Guanapay, the castle is currently referred to as the Santa Barbara Fort, and was originally constructed in the 14th century by Lanzarotto Malocello. Sites in the town which evoke its erratic history include the **Callejon de la Sandre** (Blood Alley), named after the incessant attacks by Moors and Berbers.

Palace of Queen Ico **

In the old part of the town is the Palace of Queen Ico, the most beautiful historic house in the town. It used to be the residence of the **Marquis de Herrera**, a wealthy Genoese merchant who lived here with his family during the 18th century. It is now a museum. Other places to see include the lovely old churches and convents of **San Francisco**, **Vera Cruz** and **Santo Domingo**.

> **MOUNTAIN RIDES**
>
> Many beach resorts on the islands are geared up for excursions into the interior. These can take the form of overland four-wheel-drive safaris, often organized in convoys of trucks or jeeps, making a full or half-day trek over rugged terrain. Several islands have camel, donkey and horse centres where rides are organized into the hinterland.

UNDERGROUND WONDERLAND

In the **Malpaís de La Corona**, to the north of Lanzarote, is a remarkable rock formation created by explosive volcanic gases and molten lava. This is the longest known volcanic cave in the world and was once used as a refuge from Barbary pirates. The shorter **Jameos de Agua** cave formation contains an underground salt-water lagoon and gases have penetrated the cave roof, providing natural lighting. In 1976 **César Manrique** built an 800-seat underground auditorium inside the cavern, making use of the excellent subterranean acoustics.

Opposite: *Village and palm grove of La Haria, surrounded by volcanic cones.*
Below: *Striking cacti are the star attractions of the Jardín de Cactus, created by César Manrique.*

Nuestra Señora de Gualdeloupe **

The church of Nuestra Señora de Gualdeloupe, in the centre of Teguise, is one of the oldest in the Canaries. Typically Moorish-style grand houses and mansions with ornate balconies and shady courtyards dot the town's cobbled lanes.

El Meson de Paco **

The early 18th-century El Meson de Paco is just one of these grandiose houses, and it has been converted into a restaurant and art gallery. Teguise is an extensive municipality of Lazarote and includes 20 villages.

AROUND THE NORTH

Take the route out of the capital to **Tahiche**, a town with several imposing villas. One of these was the home of the artist César Manrique and is now a museum. Turning right, the road heads north to **Guatiza**, the cochineal centre of the island. Note the huge fields of optunia cactus, grown for the raising of the insect from which the red cochineal dye is extracted. Look for the windmill which has been converted into a restaurant as there is a fascinating **Cactus Garden** there.

Further north, the village of **Mala** is also a cochineal centre, but continue north, detouring to the right to visit the charming fishing port of **Arrieta**, with its black clinker beach.

Jameos del Agua ★★★

From here, a route heads out along the coast towards the Jameos del Agua cavern and the **Cueva de los Verdes**. The caves were created about 5000 years ago by exploding volcanic gases and lava which formed tunnels from Monte Corona to the sea. These caves were used as places of refuge by pirates. Returning to the main road, continue to the village of **Ye**, a word which means 'the end of the earth'. Once the centre for the production of purple dye, extracted from the orchilla lichen, it is now famed for the fabulous viewpoints located nearby.

Mirador del Rio ★★★

The road terminates on a flat plateau in the extreme north of the island, dominated by another of César Manrique's lava creations, the Mirador del Rio. Inland, there are marvellous views of the **Monte Corona** volcanic crater, and to the north there is a panoramic view over the El Rio stretch of sea between Lanzarote and the isle of Graciosa.

Haria ★

Returning to Ye, take the route south, to pass through the **Valley of a Thousand Palms**, and Haria village. The capital of the northern province, Haria is a picturesque Moorish-style oasis, set in countryside which boasts the most palms in the entire Canary archipelago.

VIRGIN OF THE VOLCANOES

On Lanzarote the villagers of **Mancha Blanca** have celebrated the **Fiesta de La Virgen de los Volcanes** on 15 September every year since 1824. In that year, molten lava flowed from the eruption of **Las Quemadas** volcano directly towards the village. A cross now marks the spot where the 'miracle' occurred when the Virgin of Sorrows appeared to the people commanding the lava to divert. The annual celebration is held in the little **Hermitage de la Virgen de los Dolores**.

UNDERWATER LIFE

Both commercial and sports fishing is excellent off the Canary Islands, and in the stretch of water between them and the North African coast. Spearfishing and snorkelling is popular in the waters between Lanzarote and the island of Graciosa, an area great for sports. Rock bass varieties known as *cherna* and *mero*, or grouper, make particularly good sport and good eating. Restaurants will also buy *calamares* (squid) and *pulpo* (baby octopus). Out in the deeper waters, fishermen can catch swordfish, sama (seabream) or tunny, known locally as *atún*. If you're lucky you can join a short fishing excursion privately organized by the fishermen of **Caleta del Sebo**.

Above: *A typically whitewashed villa, La Haria, covered with dazzling exotic blooms.*

Riscos de Famara ★★

Heading south again, the road passes the Riscos de Famara cliffs which rise at the island's highest point, the **Penas del Chache**, 670m (2198ft) above sea level. The land around the village of **Los Valles de Santa Catalina** is a highly fertile agricultural region. The road now runs through Teguise back to Arrecife.

LA GRACIOSA

This small, oblong-shaped islet is in the Minor Archipelago, a group which includes Alegranza, Montaña Clara, and the outcrop of Infierno (Hell's Rock or the Roque del Oeste) is just 27km^2 (10½ sq miles). La Graciosa lies to the north of Lanzarote and is separated from the larger island by a narrow stretch of water known as **El Rio** (The River). Inland, the terrain is bleak and barren. Among the four mountain peaks, the highest point, the **Montaña de las Aguilas** (The Needles) rises to 266m (873ft) above sea level in the centre of Graciosa. North of this is the 157m (515ft) **Montaña Bermeja**, and in the far south is the **Montaña Amarilla** (Yellow Mountain), just 172m (564ft) high.

On the east side of the island is the harbour of **Caleta del Sebo**, facing the **Salinas del Rio** on Lanzarote. Graciosa's only other settlement, a small fishing village called **Pedro Barba**, is located in the northeast of the

---

OFF-SHORE ISLANDS

Off the northwest coast is the tiny uninhabited islet of **Montaña Clara**, projecting 256m (840ft) out of the sea. **Roque del Oeste** (Hell's Rock) is a sea pinnacle just northeast of Montaña Clara. Far out to the east of Graciosa, off the Punta Pedro Barba, is the little islet of **Roque del Este**. About 11km (7 miles) north of Lanzarote is **Alegranza**, larger, rounded, and also uninhabited. Its highest peak, after which the island is named, towers 289m (948ft) above sea level, and the islet's **Montana Lobos** (Mount of the Wolves) reaches 256m (840ft) in height.

LA GRACIOSA

island. Caleta del Sebo is over-shadowed by the **Montaña de Mojón**. The few volcanic cones on La Graciosa are surrounded by a flat, sandy plain. Around 500 people live on the island permanently. For many years the islanders depended entirely on fishing for their living. When a Canarian Governor named Garcia arrived in the 1850s. He divided the land between the inhabitants and gave them a dozen camels to boot! Since then, the Graciosans began farming what fertile land they could salvage.

Jean de Béthancourt claimed the island for the Spanish crown in 1402, when he landed there. He used this island as a military base from which he could attack the other islands. On hearing that Béthancourt's nephew, a few years later, was planning to sell La Graciosa to the Portugese, Juan II of Spain sent Pedro Barba to the island where he audaciously declared himself King of the Canaries. Cervantes refers to the incident in his novel, *Don Quixote*.

This little desert island was later to become the haunt of many pirates, with stories of buried buccaneers' treasure. The island now attracts fishermen and beach-lovers who flock to **Las Conchas** on the northwest coast, sheltered by the Montaña Bermeja, **Playa Lambra** in the north, **Playa Francesa** in the extreme south and the beach near the island's harbour.

Below: *View of Isla Graciosa from Mirador del Rio.*

AFRICA'S SHORES

From La Graciosa and Lanzarote, the shores of Morocco are just 100km (60 miles) to the east. You can make a flying visit from either Las Palmas's Gando Airport on Gran Canaria, or Reina Sofia Airport on Tenerife, to several destinations in West Africa. Morocco, Marrakesh, Casablanca, Agadir and El Aiun are the most popular destinations while excursions further abroad can be made to Nouadihbou and Nouakchott in Mauritania; to Dakar in Senegal, Libreville in Gabon and to Abijan on the Ivory Coast. There is a shipping line which takes passengers on the 18-hour sailing trip from Las Palmas to Agadir.

Lanzarote at a Glance

BEST TIMES TO VISIT

The climate varies little throughout the year, but at night, during the winter, the temperatures can drop and it may feel rather cool.

GETTING THERE

To Lanzarote: most visitors from abroad arrive by **air** at the **Arrecife Airport**. There are **ferry services** from Cádiz. **To La Graciosa:** a 40-minute **ferry** which leaves at 10:00 and returns around 16:00, runs between Orzola, at the northernmost tip of Lanzarote, and Caleta del Sebo.

GETTING AROUND

The best way to get around Lanzarote is by **car**. Petrol stations rarely accept credit cards and may be closed on Sundays. If you have brought you own car on the ferry, make sure you have the right documents. There are numerous **bus** excursions on the island with full or half day tours on offer.

WHERE TO STAY

There are only a few hotels on Lanzarote because most tourists prefer **apartment** blocks, or the cheaper **pensions**. On La Graciosa there is no official accommodation.

Arrecife
MID-RANGE
Miramar, Coll 2; tel: (928) 81 04 38, fax: 81 33 66; the facilities are basic but accommodation is near the town.

BUDGET
Cardona, Calle 18 de Julio 11; tel: (928) 81 10 08, fax: 81 70 08; comfortable pension-style accommodation offering adequate facilities.

Puerto del Carmen
LUXURY
Los Fariones, Roque del Este, 1; tel: (928) 51 01 75, fax: 51 02 02; great position, fine pool.

MID-RANGE
San Antonio, Avenida de las Playas 84; tel: (928) 51 42 00, fax: 51 30 80; quiet, 15 minutes from the airport.

Teguise
LUXURY
Gran Melia Salinas, Costa Teguise; tel: (928) 59 00 10, fax: 59 03 90; tropical-style hotel, sea views.

MID-RANGE
Occidental Teguise Playa, Avda. Jablillo, s/n; tel: (928) 59 06 54, fax: 59 09 79; private beach.

Yaiza
LUXURY
Hotel Lanzarote, Princess, Playa Blanca, Yaiza; tel: (928) 51 71 08, fax: 51 70 11; swimming pool.

MID-RANGE
Hotel Playa Flamingo, Urbanizacion Montana Roja; tel: (928) 51 73 00, fax: 51 76 42; bungalows in lovely garden location, pool, artificial beach.

Tias
LUXURY
Riu Palace Lanzarote, Playa de los Pocillos, tel: (928) 51 24 04, fax: 51 35 98; good amenities, pool.

BUDGET
Magec, Calle Hierro 8; tel: (928) 51 38 74; basic pension-style accommodation.

Apartments
Arrecife
MID-RANGE
Arrecife Playa, Avenida Mancomunidad 4; tel: (928) 81 03 00, fax: 81 39 37; quite convenient location.

BUDGET
Apartamentos Islamar, Avda. Rafael Gonzalez Negrin 15; tel: (928) 81 15 04, fax: 81 15 00; centrally located in the city on the edge of the main park.

Puerto del Carmen
LUXURY
Apartementos Flamingo Club, Avenida Las Playas; tel: (928) 51 27 53, fax: 51 43 70; great for families.

MID-RANGE
Apartamentos Morana, Guanapay 2; tel: (928) 51 01 93, fax: 51 27 24; economical, mid-1980s style.
Apartamentos Kontiki, Guanapay 5; tel: (928) 51 39 50, fax: 51 39 77; popular, central.
Apartamentos Las Panitas y Las Calas, Cla Chalana 2; tel:

Lanzarote at a Glance

(928) 51 42 62, fax: 51 42 63; central in resort.
Apartamentos Playa Club, Pedro Barba 2; tel: (928) 51 37 19, fax: 51 09 06; economical.

Where to Eat

Arrecife
Juan Carlos, Calle José Antonio 100; traditional fare.

Tias
Castillo San José, modern furnishing inside a fascinating old castle. Well worth a visit.

Puerto del Carmen
Casa Colón, Centro Comercial Matagorda; tel: (928) 51 25 54; fresh fish and traditional dishes.

Yaiza
Chu-Lin 1V, Playa Blanca; tel: (928) 51 75 67; roast pork dishes are a speciality here.

Timanfaya National Park
El Diablo; tel: (928) 84 00 56; watch dishes being cooked in the hot lava ovens.
Castillo de San José; tel: (928) 81 23 21; castle and museum with restaurant and exhibition centre. Open 11:00–21:00, daily. Restaurant opens 13:00–16:00 and 20:00–01:00.

Tours and Excursions

Jeep Excursions: most major hotels can organize jeep safaris on the island. Pick-up points are generally in the Teguise resort area, at points in the Puerto del Carmen resort and in Arrecife. Tours start between 08:30 and 09:30 depending on the pick-up point. Often the tours are in convoy. Contact Explora (tel: (928) 81 36 42), the major excursion company.
Timanfaya National Park: conducted bus tours leave from the entrance hourly, and independent visits can be made only with an authorized guide, tel: (928) 84 00 57 for the Park's organizers. Open 09:00–17:45.
Jameos del Agua: the lava grotto in the northeast of the island offers a guided tour and has a restaurant, tel: (928) 84 80 04 for details. Open 11:00–18:45 daily. For events held in the caves, it opens again 19:00–03:00 on Tues, Fri and Sat.
Cueva de los Verdes: conducted tours take visitors through this cave system in the northeast of Lanzarote every hour from 10:20 until 18:00. So popular is this attraction that it is advisable to go early as the caves quickly become far too busy; tel: (928) 17 32 20 for details.
Mirador del Rio: the observation gallery with its bar and café on the extreme northernmost point of the island overlooks La Graciosa Island. Open to visitors from 10:30 until 18:45 daily, tel: (928) 61 43 18 for further information.
Boat Trips: various excursions leave regularly from Arrecife, Puerto del Carmen and Playa Blanca. Trips can be made to the Islands of Lobos and Fuerteventura. A sailing trip offers excursions from Arrecife, down Lanzarote's east coast as far as Papagayo, in the far south and back to the port.
Coach Excursions: there are numerous coach trips which can be joined at many of the larger hotels and apartment complexes. The full day trip to Timanfaya Park is popular. This excursion also takes in the sites of El Golfo, La Geria and Yaiza. Alternatively, there is a half-day tour to the north of the island which includes Teguise, Haria, the Mirador del Rio, the Cueva de los Verdes and the Jameos del Agua. More specialist trips take visitors to see Canarian wrestling and traditional folk dancing displays at Uga or to the Teguise market on Sundays.
Sport: Tennis and watersport facilities are available at most apartment complexes and hotels. There are special centres for sports such as squash, basketball, volleyball, windsurfing and scuba diving.

Useful Contacts

Tourist Information Office, Parque José Ramírez Cerda, tel/fax: 81 18 60; Internet: www.cabildo.com
Patronato de Turismo, Antiguo Parador de Turismo, Arrecife, tel: (928) 81 17 62.
Aeropuerto de Lanzarote, Arrecife, tel: (928) 81 03 50.
IBERIA Airlines, Avenida Rafael Gonzalez 2, Arrecife, tel: (928) 81 61 08.
Betancuria Ferry, tel: (928) 51 72 66.

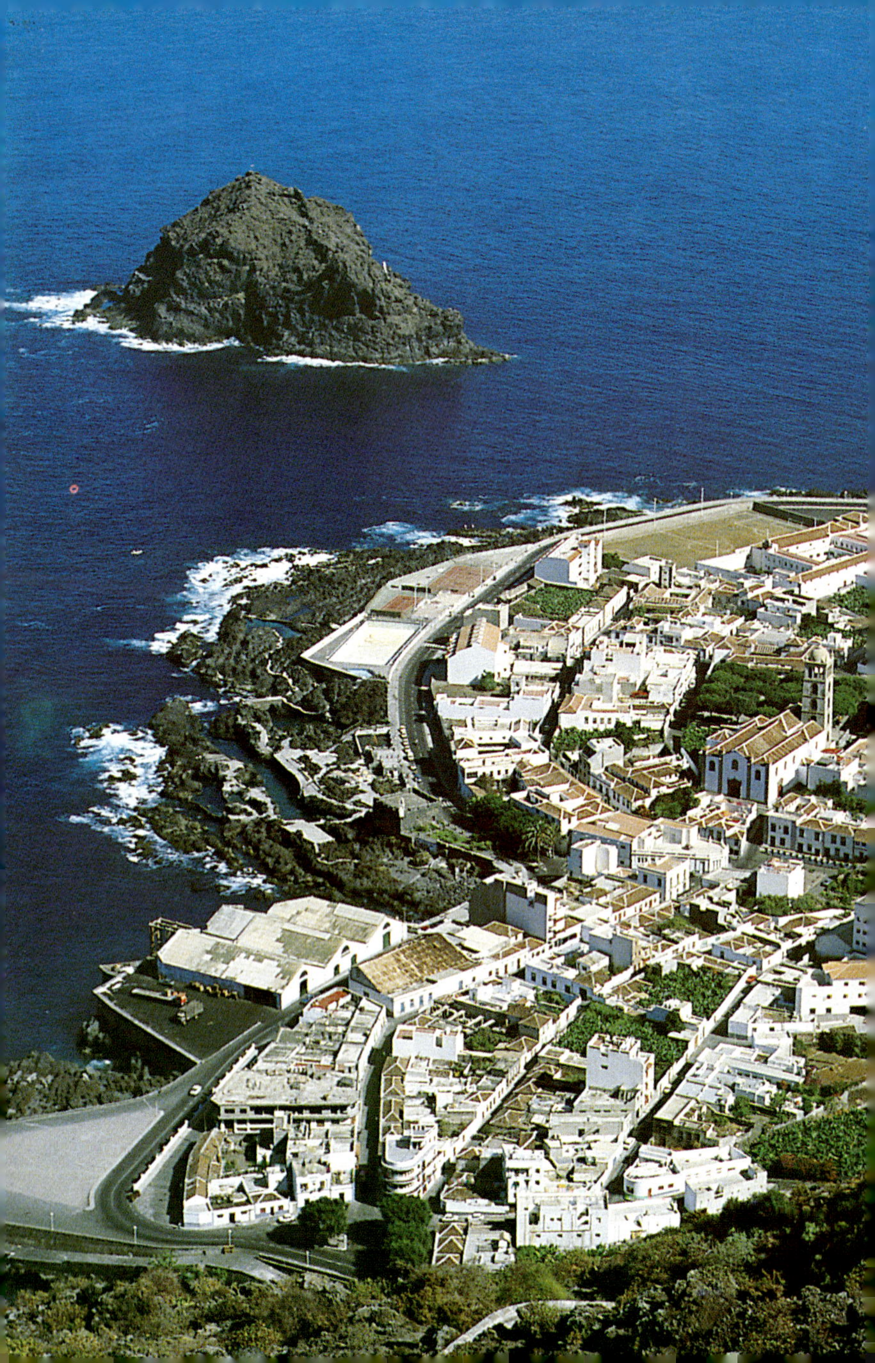

6
Tenerife

This is probably the best known of all the Canary Islands. Tenerife is the largest island in the archipelago and boasts the highest point in Spain, **Mount Teide**, which is 3718m (12,198ft) high. Locals call Tenerife the '**Island of Eternal Spring**'. Green acres of banana plantations, oranges, fields of tomatoes and, lately, other tropical fruits endorse this title, as do the green northern regions and the island's perfect climate.

A rocky spine runs down the isle to Mount Teide, which is surrounded by an enormous crater known as **Las Cañadas**; together they form Teide National Park. The volcano has been dormant as far back as 1798 and the mountain is still easily reached by road or by cable car.

The **Anaga Mountains** shelter the capital, **Santa Cruz**, on the rugged northern tip of the island. In the west are the remote **Teno Hills**. Both north and west are the most fertile and green regions, compared with the rather dull and dry southern part of Tenerife, where holidaymakers crowd onto beaches such as **Playa de las Américas** and **Los Cristianos**. Near these popular resorts is the **Costa del Silencio**, with breathtaking views of **Punta de la Rasca**, the island's southernmost point. **Las Teresitas**, north of the capital, is famous for its large artificial beach of Saharan sands.

Away from the resorts are numerous lovely old towns full of historic buildings and tranquil, leafy squares. **La Laguna**, **Orotava** and **Puerto de la Cruz** in particular are charming colonial towns.

Don't Miss

*** **La Laguna:** original settlement with many fine religious monuments and historic sites.
*** **La Orotava:** grand old town houses and a 16th-century church.
*** **Mount Teide:** highest peak in Spain and massive crater 80km (50 miles) across.
*** **Icod:** see the ancient dragon tree and views of Mount Teide.

Opposite: *Viewed across the lava-based town of Garachico is the pinnacle of the Roque de Garachico.*

TENERIFE

CRIME

Theft from cars is by far the most common crime: you can virtually guarantee having your car broken into if you park overnight in the streets of one of the big towns or resorts. Don't leave anything of value in your car, even if it is locked in the boot. If you are burgled, you'll need a report from the local police station for insurance purposes. In cities and resorts there are the usual problems of bag-snatching and occasional muggings in the seedier areas. Be as street-wise as you'd be in your own country.

SANTA CRUZ DE TENERIFE

Located on the northeast coast of Tenerife, the capital is a bustling city and major commercial and cruise ship port, quite different from anywhere else on the island. Santa Cruz is also the administrative capital of the four Western Islands of the Canaries. It is situated on a large natural bay, with a backdrop of the 1000m (3281ft) high **Anaga** mountains. A small gorge, the **Barranco de Santos,** runs through part of the city. Santa Cruz rarely holds visitors' attention for long, as most tourists head for the beach resorts or natural attractions of the countryside. The city is famous for its extravagant carnival usually held in February, depending on the dates of Lent.

The capital has over 203,000 inhabitants, roughly a third of the island's population, and it is one of Spain's busiest harbours, having attained freeport status in 1852.

It is also one of the deepest ports in the world. Today, few traces remain of the city's early history.

Tourism first started in Tenerife in 1886 when Bernard Walsh opened the **Grand Hotel** in **Puerto de la Cruz**, which is situated on the other side of the island. It was usual for tourism to start in the capital, but this was not the case for Tenerife. From the mid-19th century, the island's capital, however, became an important commercial centre. Today, most travellers to Tenerife arrive at the **Reina Sofía International Airport** in the south of the island. The city itself has many attractions, and most visitors start their tour of the city's main sights from the portside corniche.

City Sightseeing

There are several points of interest in this largely modern city. The **Plaza de España** is the main feature of the seafront and a good place to start a tour of the city; there's also a car park nearby. Towering over the circular Plaza is the **Monumento de los Caidos**, commemorating those who died in the Spanish Civil War (1936–39). The large building facing the monument is the **Palacio Insular**, the house of the government of Tenerife. The foyer has a fine relief model of the entire island, which is useful for visitors who wish to see the island in perspective and plan excursions. The **Island Tourist Board** is also located here, where you can pick up maps, street plans, information on accommodation and transport timetables.

Around the corner from the Tourist Office, the nearest museum to the Plaza de España is the **Archaeological and Anthropological Museum** situated on Avenida Bravo Murillo, on the second floor of the

> **ENTERTAINMENT**
>
> Spain is for party animals and the Canary Islands are no exception. You'll find plenty of opportunities to act as the locals do and *aplatanamiento* – 'become a banana', as the saying goes! There are nightclubs, discos and casinos, amusement arcades, countless bars, cafés and, in some areas, non-typical 'pubs'.
> The quality of entertainment varies and the action doesn't really get going till midnight. Most bars are free: you'll pay an admission charge to clubs, which usually includes the price of a drink. **Playa del Inglés** on Gran Canaria and **Playa de las Américas** on Tenerife attract a fun-seeking young and lively crowd.

Below: *The Canary Islands are well known for the excellence of their pottery and tile craftsmanship both for decorative and practical use. These benchbrick advertising plaques, in Plaza 25 Julio in Santa Cruz de Tenerife, serve both purposes.*

CHILDREN

Tenerife, Gran Canaria and Lanzarote are ideal for family holidays. Canarians love children and you'll have no problems taking them into restaurants or bars. There are plenty of watersports, waterparks, go-karts, several wildlife parks and camel or donkey rides for children to enjoy.

Palacio Insular. This museum has an excellent collection of artifacts from Guanche times. Exhibits include mummified Guanches (once stored in caves), weapons, tools, cooking utensils and early jewellery. Open 09:00–13:00 and 16:00–18:00, Monday–Friday, 09:00–13:00 Saturday, tel: (928) 60 55 74.

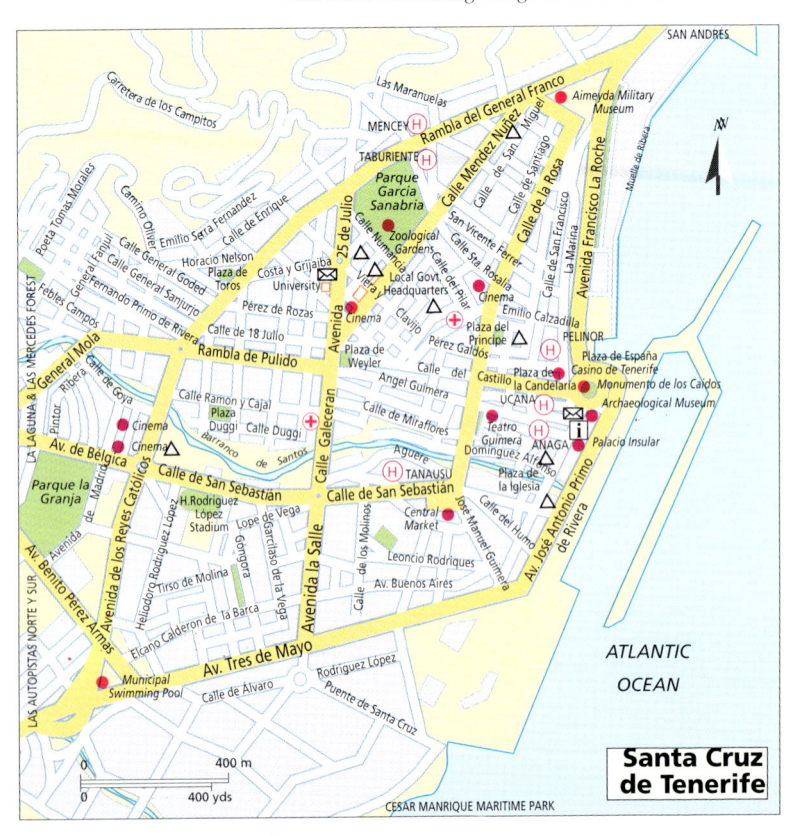

Just inland from the Plaza de España is the Plaza de Candelaria. Here the 1742 **Palacio de Carta** bank, a National Monument, is a fine example of colonial architecture. The nearby **Fine Arts Museum** is the city's main art gallery. Apart from the fabulous paintings there are also other fascinating things to see such as armour and weaponry, ship models and coins. The museum is in the Plaza del Principe, a lovely leafy square. Open 10:00–20:00 (summer) 10:00–19:00 (winter), closed Friday and Sunday, tel: (928) 24 43 58. Behind this museum, facing on to the street below, is the beautiful Baroque 17th-century **Church of San Francisco**, which was founded by exiled Irish Catholics and which contains some fine sculptures.

Crossing into Plaza del Principe, the road running north is Calle del Pilar, named after the 18th-century **Church of Pilar**, worth seeing for its beautifully painted ceiling. At the top of Calle del Pilar are the charming landscaped gardens of **Jardín Garcia Sanabria**. Sculptures line the walks, together with finely tiled benches dating back to the park's foundation in the 1920s.

To the west of the Plaza de España is the Church of **Nuestra Señora de la Concepción** on Plaza de la Iglesia. Built originally in 1502, the church was reconstructed after a fire in 1652. Its black and white tower is Moorish in influence. Inside the high Baroque interior, with its five naves, is a magnificent altarpiece, the Cross of Conquest, carried by Alonso de Lugo's men in 1494 , and the flags captured from Nelson's troops in 1797. Open 11:00–13:00, Monday-Friday. The nearby **Museum of Natural Science** is open 10:00–17:00 Tuesday–Saturday, tel: (928) 21 30 00.

Above: *The Plaza de General Weyler, decked with colourful flowerbeds.*

Military Museum *

East of the city is the **Aimeyda Barracks**. Inside this is the Military Museum. Armour and weapons are exhibited here, some dating back to the conquistadores who defeated the Guanches in 1494. The prime exhibit is *El Tigre*, the cannon which was said to have torn Nelson's arm off in his failed attack on the city in 1797. The flags from HMS *Emerald*, the Admiral's flagship, are also on display here.

GETTING THE SACK

Shakespeare's Falstaff was probably the best-known imbiber of Canarian Sack or Malvasia (Malmsey) wine. This was one of the island's main exports to Europe from the 16th to the 18th centuries. Today this wine is still served. Other wines made on Tenerife include the celebrated Vino Norte, made in El Suazal. In most shops wines from other islands, like the Vino del Monte from Gran Canaria, or Vino Herreño from El Hierro, as well as Rioja imported from Spain, are becoming much more popular than the local Sack.

Shopping

Santa Cruz is a duty-free paradise for shopaholics. Just start at the **Plaza de España** and walk through to the **Plaza de la Candeleria**. The marble statue, carved by Canova in 1778, commemorates the Virgin of Candelaria. Change your money in the beautiful **Palacio de Carta** bank. Around the square is a jumble of shops, competing in price with each other, and selling a variety of similar goods. Arts and craftwork, ceramics and souvenirs, can be bought in the shops nearby, and leather boutiques and electrical shops line both sides of the street. Off the plaza, **Calle del Castillo** is Santa Cruz's main shopping thoroughfare.

DUTY-FREE SOUVENIRS

The best bargains in Tenerife are not the electrical goods or cameras, but alcohol, tobacco and craftwork. Buy these before leaving for the airport. In the island's main markets, like the Nuestra Señora de Africa in Santa Cruz, bargaining is recommended. Food produce, like local cheeses, honey, wines, and Canarian rum make excellent gifts. Hand-made cigars are popular, as are the numerous objects and utensils made from the local terracotta. Embroidery, open-work and threadwork in the form of tablecloths, linen and aprons make truly Canarian souvenirs, as do the island's beautiful flowers, straw-work and wood carvings.

INLAND FROM SANTA CRUZ

Inland from the capital is the ancient university town of **La Laguna**, set in spectacular countryside. **La Orotava**, within a valley on the north coast, is a beautiful example of old colonial architecture and has exceptional landscaped gardens.

Puerto de la Cruz, near La Orotava, lies on the northern shores and is an important tourist resort combining both traditional old charm and modern facilities. Near Icod, on the northwest coast, is the pretty village of **Garachico**, famous for the natural rock pools of **El Caletón** and **El Puertito** and a valuable silver cross which you'll see at **San Marcos** parish church. Heading south through rugged scenery on a tortuous route passing **Santiago de Teide**, the road rises towards the coast to present a panoramic view of the **Cliffs of the Giants**. There is something in Tenerife for all visitors, from stunning expanses of black or golden sand, to the dramatic mountain scenery or the peaceful town plazas and picturesque old buildings.

La Laguna **

Just inland from Santa Cruz, in a beautiful valley, is the island's second most important town, **La Laguna**. Founded in 1496 by Alonso Fernández de Lugo, this is a university town, with an important 16th-century neo-Classical cathedral and the Church of **Nuestra Señora de la Concepción**. To the west of the town is the popular seaside resort of **El Arenal**. Nearby is **Los Rodeos** airport.

The **Santa Iglesia Cathedral** houses a vast Baroque altarpiece, La Virgin de los Remedios, a silver altar, fine Flemish works of art, an English organ, and a 1767 marble pulpit. The 16th-century Church of Nuestra Señora de la Concepción has a fine Mudéjar carved wooden ceiling and an exceptional Baroque wooden pulpit from the 18th century. Said to be the island's most beautiful church, it has a six-tiered tower and three naves.

Until 1723, Laguna was the island's capital. Laguna boasts a string of fine religious buildings such as the 17th-century **Bishop's Palace**, monasteries, hermitages, convents (such as those of San Francisco and Santa Catalina) and palaces like **La Nava**, and its huge ancient dragon tree, located in the Seminary Gardens.

Around the north coast of the island is the site of the defeat of the native Guanches by the Spanish in 1494. The pretty village of **El Sauzal**, the **Playa del Roque**, the **Bajamar** clifftop resort and the **Hidalgo Point** are also interesting places to visit. To the north of Santa Cruz there are several sights surrounding the **Anaga mountain range** which rises up to 1000m (3281ft).

BARS AND CAFÉS

Bars and cafés form an important part of Canarian culture. Open from sunrise to the small hours, they're fairly spartan and male-dominated. As in the rest of Spain the decibel level is high. Order a drink and you can stay as long as you like. Prices are lower at the bar than if you occupy a table: pay as you leave and don't forget to tip.

Below: *A storm rages over Puerto de la Cruz, a resort that has preserved its colonial grandeur.*
Opposite: *The city museums, art galleries and exhibition halls of Santa Cruz are housed in ornate buildings.*

> **THREE CENTURIES OF TOURISM**
>
> With a current population of around 665,000, many of whom are either German, English or Indian, the island became a tourist attraction as early as the 18th century. The celebrated German naturalist, Alexander von Humbolt, was enthralled by the island when he visited it in 1799. It has charmed visitors ever since. In 1892, Spain's largest tourist hotel, the Taoro, was built in Orotava and it is now a casino. Since then, tourism on the island has boomed.

Below: *In 1975, four million sacks of Saharan sand were transported to Las Teresitas to create this beach north of Santa Cruz.*

Las Mercedes **

A steep, gullied sierra conceals the beautiful Las Mercedes forest, a botanist's paradise and packed with fascinating flora. The dense forests and jagged mountain scenery are best viewed from the **Pico del Inglés** mirador. On a clear day there's a breathtaking panorama of rugged peaks, rolling hills and the crystal-clear water of the Atlantic ocean to the north.

Northeast of the mirador, **Taganana** is a picturesque little village on the coast with good beaches nearby. Down the other side of the Anaga mountain chain is the fishing village of **San Andrés**, with its golden sand beach of **Las Teresitas**, just 5km (3 miles) north of the capital. Las Teresitas is a lovely artificial beach that is virtually deserted out of high season.

Tacoronte *

Tacoronte is famous for its wine and you can sample a glass or two in a local *bodega* (wine cellar). The highlight of this market town is the old Augustinian monastery, whose chapel houses the 17th-century **Cristo de los Dolores**, a statue modelled on an engraving by the great German Renaissance artist Albrecht Dürer, which is well worth seeing.

La Orotava ***

Probably one of the prettiest towns on Tenerife, **La Orotava** is an architectural jewel, with many magnificent historic buildings and some cobbled streets. It's an old town but very well preserved.

Among Orotava's many interesting sites are the 18th-century Baroque **La Concepción Church**. It has a beautiful carved ceiling, as well as images and paintings from the 16th century. Other sites worth seeing include **San Juan** and the **Hermitage of El Calvario**.

Above: Over 4000 species of plant in Puerto de la Cruz's Botanical Gardens originated in Africa, Asia and America.

Don't miss the **Museo de Artesania Ibero-Americana** within **Santo Domingo Convent** (la Casa de los Balcones), a masterpiece of traditional woodworking skills dating from 1632. Further up the hill, opposite the 18th-century **Hospital de la Trinidad**, there is a beautiful park and a 17th-century mill. You will see the most spectacular views of Puerto de la Cruz from Humboldt's viewpoint at La Cuesta de la Villa, on the outskirts of La Orotava.

Botanical Gardens of Acclimatization ★★

Take the road west from La Orotava to Puerto de la Cruz until you reach the 1788 Botanical Gardens of Acclimatization. The aim of this garden was to acclimatize plants and trees to the Canarian climate and then move them to the Spanish mainland. There is an astonishing variety of beautiful plants, trees and shrubs from all over the world. Open 09:00–19:00 April–September, 09:00–18:00 October–March, closed Good Friday, 25 December and New Year. Tel: (928) 38 35 72.

Puerto de la Cruz ★★

One of the top resorts in the Canary Islands, Puerto de la Cruz is a lively, atmospheric town with a fascinating history. Known locally as 'Puerto', its early prosperity

---

FUN AND GAMES

Children will love **Loro Parque**, home to hundreds of brightly coloured parrots and friendly dolphins. It's just on the outskirts of Puerto de la Cruz and there are regular live shows to be enjoyed. Also great for children is **Zoolandia** on the eastern outskirts of Puerto – an interesting and humane zoo.
Adults should stop off at the **Bananera el Guanche**, off the Orotava road, a working plantation that gives a fascinating insight into how bananas are cultivated. More hedonistic thrill-seekers can head for Puerto's **casino** in the town itself and try their luck at the gaming wheels.

was based on the export of sugar and wine; later, cochineal and bananas. More recently, Puerto has been welcoming tourists, ever since the **Grand Hotel** was opened far back in 1886.

The main square, **Plaza Charco**, is the focal point for visitors and locals alike, who relax in the numerous bars and restaurants. There's a lovely old town just off the Plaza Charco around the fishing port, **Puerto Pesquero**, which is full of narrow, cobbled streets packed with imposing colonial architecture.

Above: *Magnificent Mount Teide, often covered in snow is the highest point in all Spanish territory.*

SPAIN'S HIGHEST PEAK

The **Caldera**, or Cauldron, of Teide, was formed 300,000 years ago, and the peak of **Mount Teide** pushed up 3718m (12,198ft) through the earth's crust in around 200,000BC. The National Park of Teide was created in 1954. Many rare plants and bird species are found in this natural wonderland. A cable car takes visitors up almost to the crater's rim to see Teide's Peak, which is snow-covered in winter. Strict regulations prevent the removal of plants or rocks from the park.

The National Park of Teide ★★★

Inland from La Orotava, take a trip into the **Cañadas del Teide** which dominates the island. From **El Portillo de Las Cañadas** (the Gateway) where there is a park and Visitor's Centre, a route runs east across the wonderful **La Esperanza Forest**, and the first mountain reached on this route, after Aguamansa, **Monte Verde** (Green Mountain), is aptly named as it is a botanical paradise. At **Las Raíces**, in a clearing in La Esperanza Forest, an obelisk commemorates General Franco's secret meeting in June 1936, where he carefully planned his military coup. Visit the fabulous caves called the **Cueva del Hielo**, to the right of the path, in order to see the ice stalactites.

The focus of the national park is its vast crater, called the Caldera de las Cañadas. Mount Teide is no more than a large cone lying on the edge of this crater which is even more spectacular than Teide itself. Teide National Park can be approached from **La Esperanza** village, to the north, from La Orotava to the west and also from **Boca del Tauce** in the south.

THE COAST

The Coast

Among the many places to explore along Tenerife's north coast are the quaint old towns of Icod de Los Viños and San Marcos, while on the east coast you will come across the fascinating historic town of Garachico.

Icod de Los Viños ★★★

One of Tenerife's oldest towns, Icod lies on the island's north coast. Although it was founded by the Spanish in 1501, it was originally a Guanche settlement. Here is a famous dragon tree, said to be 1000 years old although the real age of this tree remains unknown. There are numerous religious monuments and churches, such as the convent of **San Agustín** and the beautiful Renaissance church of **San Marcos** on El Pilar Square.

San Marcos ★

The nearby village of San Marcos is small and quiet and a good place to get away from the crowds for a short while. Originally a fishing port, San Marcos is now becoming a popular resort, largely due to its beautiful beaches, excellent fish restaurants and lively bars.

Garachico ★★

Situated on Tenerife's northwestern shore, Garachico is a historic town which escaped the fury of Mount Teide's eruption in 1706. The town is filled with notable

> **LAND OF MIRADORS**
>
> One of the best views of Mount Teide is from the **Mirador Margarita Diedra**, on the road out of Orotava. The **Valley of Ariba Mirador** also offers stunning views of the mountain up through the **Ariba Valley**. The road up to the peak from La Laguna has many miradors, the **Pico de la Flores**, **El Diablillo**, the **Mirador of Ortuno** and the **Mirador Ayosa**.

Below: *Tenerife is a botanists' paradise with carpets of flowers during springtime.*

Above: *Garachico has many fine buildings in the process of being restored.*

WATERSPORTS

Watersports dominate the Canary Islands, with windsurfing being the most popular. You can rent scuba-diving equipment, sailboards, boats and jet skis at the major resorts. Surfers ride the waves at **Playa de Martianez** on Tenerife and **Maspalomas** on Las Palmas. For swimming, most resort beaches are safe, but do be careful on all other beaches: there may be dangerous undertows.

old buildings which include the palace of the counts of Gomera, the 1575 **San Miguel Castle** and, the **Santa Ana Church**, which houses works by the Canarian sculptor, José Lujan Pérez, and the convent of **San Francisco**. Currently, many of the town's fine buildings are being carefully restored. Located on an arc of land at the bottom of a volcanic valley, the town faces the weirdly shaped **Roque de Garachico**. Natural rock pools, which have been formed by the lava, have been converted into bathing pools of crystal-clear sea water. The port here was once the island's main harbour for agricultural exports.

Moving around the coast to the west side of the island, **Puerto del Santiago** is well-known for the nearby **Cliffs of the Giants**. The town has a wide bay and a large yacht harbour, and is fast becoming an upmarket resort. Near **Playa de la Arena** there is a beach of black volcanic sand.

Playa de las Américas and Los Cristianos *

These adjacent resorts are the most popular places in Tenerife. Year-round sunshine and a wealth of watersports and boat trips act as a magnet for hundreds of thousands of happy holidaymakers. **Playa de las Américas** has been unashamedly developed for fun in the sun. You won't find much traditional Canarian – or Spanish – culture here but there's plenty of boisterous nightlife and you won't have to look hard to find an English-style pub or a plate of fish and chips. **Los Cristianos** was once a tiny fishing village and retains traces of its original charm, particularly around the old harbour. Families should head for **Aguapark Octopus** nearby to brave the thrilling waterslides.

Heading east, the **Costa del Silencio** shelters a few small resorts like **Las Galletas**, with its Amarilla Golf and Country Club. The east coast leading back to Santa Cruz is peppered with lovely sheltered beaches. **Candelaria**, a few kilometres before the capital, is a world-famous place of pilgrimage. The town is dominated by an impressive basilica that houses a statue of Tenerife's patron saint, Nuestra Señora de la Candelaria.

THE BLACK MADONNA

In 1826, the statue of the Black Madonna of Candelaria, Tenerife's patron saint, was carried out to sea, from where it is said to have originated, by a huge tidal wave, and replaced by a copy which stands in the impressively spired basilica. Thousands of pilgrims congregate in Candelaria each year on 14 and 15 August.

Below: *The Basilica of Candelaria is one of Tenerife's most important pilgrimage attractions, housing a copy of an original statue of the Virgin which dated from the 1300s.*

Tenerife at a Glance

BEST TIMES TO VISIT

Named Tenerife after the Guanche words for 'White Mountain', the Canaries' largest island's name celebrates the Teide Peak that dominates Tenerife. To the north, where the capital is located, the island is green and often overcast or cloudy. In the arid south, the weather is more often sunny and cloudless. The weather, on the whole, is usually pleasant wherever you are on Tenerife.

GETTING THERE

Most visitors arrive by air at **Reina Sofía International Airport**. The nearest airport to Santa Cruz is **Los Rodeos** domestic airport. There are a number of **ferry services** which depart from Cádiz.

GETTING AROUND

A good **motorway** runs around the island from Puerto de la Cruz in the north, through Santa Cruz, down the east coast and along the south to Los Cristianos. A secondary **road** connects Los Cristianos with Puerto de la Cruz around the west side of the island making a coastal circumnavigation of Tenerife possible. Most roads on this island are well-surfaced.

WHERE TO STAY

Santa Cruz
LUXURY
Mency, Calle José Naveiras 38; tel: (922) 27 67 00, fax: 28 00 17; exquisitely furnished in Louis Quatorze style.

MID-RANGE
Colón Rambla, Viera y Clavijo 49; tel: (922) 27 25 50, fax: 27 27 16; good situation, pool.

BUDGET
Taburiente, Dr. José Naveiras 24-A; tel: (922) 27 60 00, fax: 27 05 62; impressive range of facilities for a two-star rating.
Hotel Atlantico, Calle del Castillo 12; tel: (922) 24 63 75; central location.

Puerto de la Cruz
LUXURY
Meliá Botánico, Calle RJ Yeoward; tel: (922) 38 14 00, fax: 38 15 04; beautiful gardens.

MID-RANGE
Melia Puerto de la Cruz, Villanueva del Prado; tel: (922) 38 40 11, fax: 38 65 59; excellent central location.
El Tope, Calzada de Martianez 2, tel: (922) 38 50 52, fax: 38 00 03; near beach and town.

BUDGET
Bambi, Lomito 15; tel: (922) 38 45 51, fax: 38 34 24; not far from the beach.

La Orotava
MID-RANGE
Hotel Victoria, Calle de H. Apolinar 8; tel: (922) 33 16 83; restored 15th-century mansion.

Playas de las Américas
LUXURY
Gran Hotel Playa de Duque; tel: (922) 71 00 00; 19th-century Canary village style.

Sol Elite Tenerife, Playas de las Américas; tel: (922) 79 10 62; fax: 79 39 20, near the beach.

MID-RANGE
Park Club Europe, Avenida Maritima; tel: (922) 79 26 90; fax: 79 33 52, beach nearby.

BUDGET
Oro Negro, tel: (922) 79 06 12; pool, near the beach.

Los Cristianos
LUXURY
Paradise Park, Oasis del Sur; tel: (922) 79 47 62, fax: 79 48 59; wonderful views.

MID-RANGE
Hotel Princesa Dacil, Camino Penetración; tel: (922) 75 30 30, fax: 79 06 58; three stars.

BUDGET
Andrea's, Avenida Valle Menendez, s/n D.P. 38650; tel: (922) 79 00 12, fax: 79 42 70; central, cozy, basic facilities.

Bajamar
MID-RANGE
Nautilus, Avda. de las Piscinas 2, Bajamar; tel: (922) 54 05 00.

Realejo Alto
LUXURY
Maritim, Calle Burgado 1, tel: (922) 34 20 12; fax: 34 21 09; inland but very good location.

MID-RANGE
Bahia Praque, La Longuera, tel: (922) 38 04 00; fax: 34 31 98; three-star hotel.

Tenerife at a Glance

WHERE TO EAT

Garachico
BUDGET
Il Giardino, Calle Esteban de Ponte 8; tel: (922) 83 02 45; old house in the village.

Las Canadas
LUXURY
Parador Nacional Las Canadas del Tiende; tel: (922) 38 64 15, fax: 38 64 15; built like a ski chalet with balconies. Good local food.

Santa Cruz
La Riviera, Rambla General Franco 155; tel: (922) 27 58 12; said to serve the best food on Tenerife.
El Coto de Antonio, Calle General Goded 13; tel: (922) 27 21 05; wide variety of international cuisine.
La Estancia, Calle Mendez Nuñez 110; tel: (922) 27 20 49; local specialities.

La Orotava
Restaurante Sabor Canario, Calle del Escultor Estévenez 17; imaginative local dishes.

Playas de las Américas
Bistro, Edificio Vina del Mar; tel: (922) 79 07 18; good, inexpensive cuisine.
Borinquen Tropic, Edificio Borinquen; tel: (922) 79 00 08; typical local dishes.

Puerto de la Cruz
Marquesa, Quintana, fax: (922) 38 69 50; good fare on balcony overlooking square.

Castillo San Felipe, Avenida Luis Lavaggi; tel: (922) 38 21 13; international and local dishes.
Bodega La Muralla, Calle La Holla 40; tel: (922) 38 23 01; exquisite *tapas* and small economically priced dishes.

Los Cristianos
El Sol, Chez Jaques, Calle El Cabezo; tel: (922) 70 05 69; French flavour to local dishes.
El Rancho de Don Antonio, Calle Juan XXIII; tel: (922) 79 00 92; good steak dishes.

TOURS AND EXCURSIONS

Ceramic Museum, Puerto de la Cruz; open 10:00–18:00, Sundays 10:00–13:00.
Archaeological Museum, tel: (922) 20 93 17;
Anthropology Museum, tel: (922) 20 93 20; both open 10:00–20:00, Tuesday–Sunday.
Museo Municipal de Bellas Artes, open 10:00–20:00 Monday–Saturday.
Botanical Gardens of Acclimatization, Puerto de la Cruz; tel: (922) 38 35 72. Open 09:00–18:00; closed on Good Friday, 25 December and New Year.
Parrot Park, Puerto de la Cruz, open 08:30–17:00 daily; tel: (922) 37 40 81.

Bananera El Guanche, La Orotava; tel: (922) 33 18 53, open 08:30–13:00 and 14:00–18:30 daily.
Eagles of Teide Park, Los Cristianos, Arona, open 09:00–18:00.
Medieval Night, San Miguel Castle, tel: (922) 70 02 76, open 20:00 till late.
Canelo Centre, El Tanque, tel: (922) 13 33 93, open 10:00–18:00.
La Rosaleda Rose Park, Puerto de la Cruz, open 09:00–13:00.
Yellow Submarine, Las Galletas, tel: (922) 71 50 80, open 14:00–17:00.
Cabildo Insular de Tenerife, Palacio Insular, Plaza España, Santa Cruz, tel: (922) 60 55 00/92.

USEFUL CONTACTS

Tourist Information Centre, Plaza de la Iglesia, Puerto de la Cruz, tel: (922) 38 60 00; www.puertocruzturismo.org
Airports: Los Rodeos (North), tel: (922) 25 77 45 or 63 58 00; for bookings, tel: (922) 25 23 40. Iberia, tel: 77 13 75.
Reina Sofía (South), tel: (922) 77 00 54. Iberia, tel: 77 13 75.
Gomera Ferry, Los Cristianos, tel: (922) 97 02 15.

WEST CANARY ISLANDS	J	F	M	A	M	J	J	A	S	O	N	D
AVERAGE TEMP. °C	18	18	19	19	21	22	25	25	24	23	21	19
AVERAGE TEMP. °F	64	64	66	66	70	72	77	77	75	73	70	66
HOURS OF SUN DAILY	6	7	7	8	9	10	11	10	8	7	6	6
DAYS OF RAINFALL	7	6	5	4	2	1	1	1	2	6	10	9
RAINFALL mm	36	8	2	11	2	0	0	0	6	3	58	9
RAINFALL in	1.5	0	0	0.5	0	0	0	0	0	0	2	0

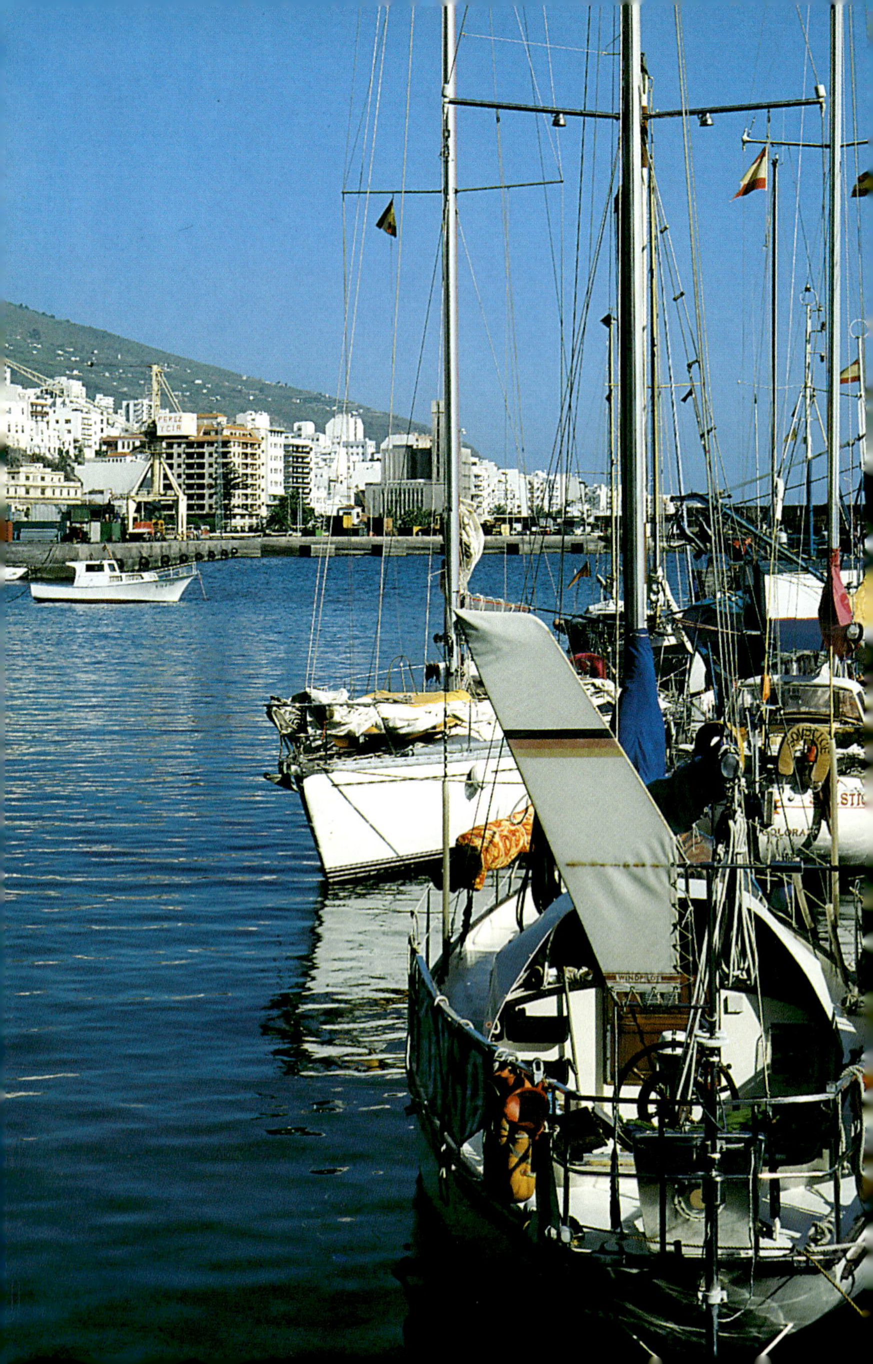

7
La Palma

With possibly the most beautiful mountain scenery in the whole of the Canary Islands, and known as 'La Isla Bonita' (the pretty island), La Palma is peaceful and unspoilt. In relation to its total area, it is one of the steepest islands in the world. Almond trees cloak La Palma with clouds of scented blossom in springtime and banana plantations cling precariously to its steep slopes.

The island itself is pear-shaped, with a rocky coast and a few good beaches. Although mostly green and fertile, the northern part of La Palma is dominated by the craggy **Roque de los Muchachos**, 2426m (7959ft) high. This looms over the **Caldera de Taburiente**, one of the world's largest volcanic craters, which is now a spectacular national park. The whole island is actually ideal for hiking and there's a wonderful variety of scenery to explore.

Santa Cruz is the capital of La Palma, a small, atmospheric city whose historic buildings help it to maintain its colonial charm, complemented by lively cafés and good restaurants. The wealth that was made from the days when the island was heavily involved in trade with the Americas is reflected in these grand old buildings. Also dotted around the island are numerous picturesque villages such as **San Andrés** and **Los Llanos de Aridane**. Most visitors to the island come to enjoy its natural beauty, but sun-lovers will find several good beaches, particularly the fine black sands of **Puerto de Naos** and **Puerto de Tazacorte** on the southwest coast.

DON'T MISS

*** La Cumbrecita: viewpoint overlooking the Caldera de Taburiente.
*** Santa Cruz: wonderful natural beauty and beaches.
** International Astrophysical Observatory: finest window on universe.
** Bosque de Los Tilos: UNESCO-protected forest.
** Fuencaliente: the island's southernmost point with two volcano cones.
** Puerto de Naos: with its fine black sand, the island's best beach.

Opposite: *The elegant old colonial port of Santa Cruz de la Palma edges the large harbour and yacht basin.*

POLICE

There are three types of police on the islands: the **Policía Municipal,** who are dressed in blue and direct traffic; the **Policía Nacional,** in brown, who look after urban areas and tourist trouble; and the **Guardia Civil**, in green, who look after the rural areas and everything else. Spanish police have a reputation for being rather uncooperative and trigger-happy but as long as you stay on the right side of the law there's no reason why you should have any trouble.

Santa Cruz de la Palma

This important port is built in an amphitheatre shape overlooking the sea on the slopes of **La Caldereta** volcanic crater. It is located on the eastern side of the heart-shaped island, about halfway down the coastline. The main part of the city, founded in 1493, is clustered around the large harbour and yacht basin which is edged by a corniche known as the **Avenida Marítima**. Almost 20,000 people inhabit this pretty, restful city of whitewashed buildings and red-tiled roofs, which cascade down the steep hillsides along winding, narrow streets.

Santa Cruz de la Palma has not, in fact, really suffered a 'sea change' with the advent of tourism like many of the capitals of other Canarian islands. Not being the main port of entry to the island, it has retained its old-world colonial grace and elegance, unspoilt by shops and high-rise hotels.

The tall building dominating the harbour is the island government's council building, the **Cabildo Insular**. One main road, the Avenida Marítima, runs south to north through the city. It sports some of the most elegant Canarian architecture on the island, its beautiful old buildings, with typical one- and two-storied balconies, have intricate wooden railings and ornate carved panels embellished with family coats-of-arms. These face the sea front and their wooden balconies are echoed in the island's **National Parador** hotel.

Further north is the 16th-century **Castillo de Santa Catalina** which defended the city against the pirates, after the repulse of an attack by Francis Drake in 1595. It is open only on special occasions.

Just past the Naval Centre is a replica in concrete of Columbus's flagship, the *Santa María*. Columbus never actually visited La Palma, but this replica is used as a maritime museum which is known locally as the **Barco de la Virgen**. Open 09:30–14:00 Monday–Friday (summer), also 16:00–19:00 (winter), closed Saturday and Sunday.

Santa Cruz city has a wonderful **Museum of Natural History and Ethnology.** It is one of the best in the Canaries, and contains a wealth of information on the islands' fauna and flora, as well as housing a number of interesting zoological examples from the island's interior. The museum is housed in a restored 16th-century convent.

Next door to the museum is the **Fine Arts Gallery**, which has an interesting collection of Spanish and Flemish paintings. Open 09:00–14:00 and 16:00–18:30, daily.

Back in the city centre, the main shopping thoroughfare is known as **Calle O'Daly**, after an Irish businessman. Numerous small shops, cafés and restaurants line the street, interspersed with some fine, old, typically Canarian houses, built around shady courtyards which can be glimpsed through the wide doorways.

Above: *Traditional whitewashed and modern buildings line Santa Cruz de La Palma's steep and narrow streets.*

MUSEUMS AND CHURCHES

Most museums and churches are closed to the public during festivals and on Sundays. Many churches post the times of their religious services on the door or gateway: visitors should respect these times when sightseeing and make sure they are properly dressed – no micro skirts, exposed shoulders or shorts. Sometimes it is necessary to find a museum curator to open a monument or historic building. Many houses on the islands which are architecturally important are often privately owned and therefore not open to the public.

ISLAND CELEBRATIONS

Every five years, the jewelled statue of **Nuestra Señora de las Nieves** is carried from Las Nieves church to Santa Cruz in a procession known as **La Bajada de la Virgen**. The Virgin is the island's patron saint. In another La Palma celebration, called the **Carnaval Blanca**, poor emigrants, who returned wealthy from the West Indies and Venezuela, are imitated in a costume parade. The rich, white Palmeros brought slaves back with them, a status symbolized by the participants whitening their faces with talcum powder, or darkening their faces to represent the coloured servants.

San Salvador Church **

The city centre proper is the **Plaza de España**, bordered by the Renaissance-style parish church of **San Salvador**, the tall bell tower of which dominates the square. The church has a fine Mudéjar coffered wooden ceiling, and the altarpiece is a depiction of the Transfiguration by the 19th-century artist Antonio Maria Esquivel. The sacristy contains some fine Gothic woodwork and the church's altar is also exquisitely carved. The statue outside the **Real Convento** (Royal Convent) of the Immaculate Conception is that of Felipe II, from whose reign the building dates.

The stone fountain, in Plaza de España which is rather impressive but non-functioning, dates from 1776, and the nearby **Cabañas Palace**, which is open during office hours, is a delightful example of contemporary wood and stone architecture.

Town Hall **

The grand colonades to one side of the plaza are those of the historic Town Hall (*Ayuntamiento*) which is also open during office hours. Dating from the 16th century, this was once the Cardinal's palace and inside are murals by Mariano de Cossio as well as lovely, dark Canarian wood panelling. Outside, the four columns of the Town Hall's façade support a typically fenestrated upper floor, decorated with a plaque of Felipe II of Spain, the La Palma coat of arms and those of the Austrian Royal Household. This triangular 'square' which is made up of the Plaza de España and the Calle O' Dally, is the centre of city life in Santa Cruz. For a relaxing coffee, try the **Café La Placeta**, in the small square of Avenida Pérez de Brito. The **Salazar Palace** is just a short walk south.

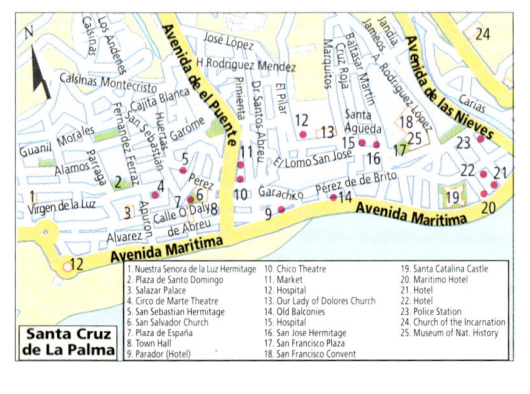

Santa Cruz de La Palma

1. Nuestra Senora de la Luz Hermitage
2. Plaza de Santo Domingo
3. Salazar Palace
4. Circo de Marte Theatre
5. San Sebastian Hermitage
6. San Salvador Church
7. Plaza de España
8. Town Hall
9. Parador (Hotel)
10. Chico Theatre
11. Market
12. Hospital
13. Our Lady of Dolores Church
14. Old Balconies
15. Hospital
16. San Jose Hermitage
17. San Francisco Plaza
18. San Francisco Convent
19. Santa Catalina Castle
20. Maritimo Hotel
21. Hotel
22. Hotel
23. Police Station
24. Church of the Incarnation
25. Museum of Nat. History

Above: *Gaily painted old colonial houses with wooden balconies in Santa Cruz.*

Tobacos Vargas *
For an interesting detour, visit the Tobacos Vargas on Avenida Maritima. Here you can see workers rolling the Palmero cigars by hand, and you'll be able to purchase some of the product which is said to rival those produced in Cuba. The cigar industry here was the result of regular migration between La Palma and Cuba.

TOURING THE ISLAND
Just outside Santa Cruz, to the north, is the 17th-century Sanctuary of the island's patron saint, **Nuestra Señora de Las Nieves** (Our Lady of the Snows), set in wooded mountain scenery.

Overshadowing the church, which contains an altar made of 18kg (40lb) of Mexican silver, is the **Pico de Las Nieves,** a fine lookout. South from this is the **Mirador la Concepción,** with fine views of the city. The island's longest tunnel leads to the turn off for **La Cumbrecita** (Little Summit), part of the Cumbre mountain spine, which stands 1833m (6014ft) high. You'll see the vast crater rim of the **Caldera de Taburiente** from the lookout here, the nearby **Loma das Chozas** and the great spire of rock rising 800m (2625ft) from the crater floor known as **Idafe Rock**.

A TYPICAL TOWN HALL

The Casa Consistoriates, Ayuntamiento, or Town Hall, on Santa Cruz's Plaza de España, is one of the finest examples of its kind in the Canaries. It was built in typically ornate style during 1563.

The Coat of Arms of San Miguel de la Palma, the island's true name, is emblazoned on the front of the elegant building, which contains some exquisite wood carvings, frescos by Cossio, and some rare treasures dating from the 16th and 17th centuries. Be sure to see the extravagant staircase, the Banqueting Hall and the Mayor's Office.

MALMSEY WINE

This strong, full-flavoured fortified white wine is known as **Malvasia** or Malmsey, after the grape it is made from. It was made initially only on **Tenerife**, and became popular throughout Europe and the Americas between the 16th and 17th centuries, when it was known as **Sack** (possibly after the Spanish word *saca* for exported goods). Much of the Malvasia wine now comes from **Lanzarote**, particularly from the region around **La Geria**. The largest wine-producing area of the Canaries is still northern Tenerife. Muscatel is another of the famous Canarian wines, and a unique wine made from laurel berries on El Hierro is known as *vino herreño*.

The main road now leads west to the island's second largest settlement, **Los Llanos**. This is the market town for the island's main agricultural region, specializing in bananas, dates and almonds. Worth a visit is **Nuestra Señora del Los Remedios**, a little 1517 church on Plaza de España. Continuing west, through Argual, a detour should be made to the **Mirador of Time** which is 594m (1949ft) high. From the lookout on the island's most picturesque valley, **Aridane**, you can see the spectacular **Gorge of Angustias**. Returning to the main road, turn down into **Tazacorte**, overlooking the shipping harbour of Puerto de Tazacorte. Tazacorte was the site of the murder of a Jesuit missionary, Fra Azevedo, who was killed by pirates in 1570, and is commemorated in the **House of the Martyrs** in the village. Puerto Tazacorte is where the conquistador Alonso Fernández de Lugo landed in 1492. From Puerto Tazacorte, take a boat trip to the spectacular **Cueva Bonita**, a cave with eerie lighting effects. Heading north, the town of **Tijarafe** is known for its 16th-century altar in the **Church of Candeleria**. Just before **Puntagorda**, there is a fine lookout for coastal views. After **Briestas** village, a turning right leads up to a mirador on the brooding, mist-shrouded **Roque de los Muchachos**, the island's highest point.

Right: *Islanders celebrate the festival of Nuestra Señora de las Nieves, when the jewelled statue of the Virgin is carried from Las Nieves to Santa Cruz.*
Opposite: *The National Park of La Caldera de Taburiente, caused by the death of a volcano, is now home to rare flora.*

National Park of La Caldera de Taburiente ★★★

The gem at the heart of La Palma island is the National Park of La Caldera de Taburiente. The Caldera, or 'cauldron' is not, as many believe, a volcanic crater. About 400,000 years ago, the massive peak of an extinct volcano collapsed inward, creating one of the largest natural bowls in the world at 9km (5½ miles) in diameter. The 'death' of the volcano extinguished any further volcanic activity in the entire area. The earth-shattering collapse caused a dent in the rim extending to the southwest. This acted as an outlet for the two rivers which converged to form the **Rio de Las Angustias** which currently has its outflow near Puerto de Tazacorte on the island's west coast.

Declared a national park in 1954, this vast depression, dominating the northern half of La Palma, rises to its highest point, the **Roque de los Muchachos,** at 2426m

---

EXOTIC FRUITS

The Canary Islands have the perfect climate for growing a variety of fruits and exotic plants. Some plants are grown commercially such as tobacco from Cuba; bananas from Africa and India; sugar cane from India; and the Strelizia (Bird of Paradise) flower from South Africa. Others are grown more as a novelty. The Mexican *zapote* tree, from which chewing gum comes; cherimoya, (custard apple), papaya, pineapple and avocado all come from Central America. The peri-melon comes from Peru, as well as kiwi and passion fruit.

Above: *The world-famous International Astrophysical Observatory is home to Europe's largest telescope.*

GOING BANANAS

La Palma is aptly described as the 'Green Island' of the Canaries as it is the most luxuriant. Contributing to the island's greenery, bananas were introduced as an important crop from Indo-China in the late 19th century. The life cycle of the banana begins at one year old when the first flowers, the female part of the hermaphrodite plant, appear. The male part is the tip of the flower stalk and pollination is not involved in the development of the fruit. Petals protect the ripening fruit which is exposed to the sun by hand, and is ready for harvesting within six or seven months.

(7959ft). On the road to the peak you will pass the **International Astrophysical Observatory** which was opened in 1985. The observatory is situated on La Palma for a reason: its geographical location and the excellent climatic conditions do not interfere with astrophysical observations. The clear air and cloudless nights were found to be ideal for astronomy, and the Swedes even built a special 'sun tower' here housing instruments used in observing the sun. The main building houses Europe's largest telescope. It is one of the most important observatories in the world, and several countries contributed to its foundation. The Observatory Roque de los Muchachos is reached by a new track from Miranda (visits only by arrangement).

The remoteness of the island and its lack of development means that the observatory is free from distracting artificial light. The shape of the mountain and the prevailing winds also means that the airflow remains undisturbed. From January to March snow lies on the crater rim and it can be cold at these heights. The observatory is situated quite high up, above the clouds for most of the year. This is rather convenient as clouds trap dust and moisture whch interferes with the airflow.

TOURING THE ISLAND

As one of the most important parks in Spain, not only for its spectacular scenery but because of its precious and unique flora, the Caldera is managed by ICONA, the national forestry agency. ICONA, together with the UNESCO biosphere programme, is also responsible for La Palma's other unique natural feature, the **Los Tilos** forest in the northeast of the island which contains many of the lovely 'laurisilva' trees. In each site, the organizations have an information and ecological research centre.

The information centre of the **Caldera de Taburiente** is located at the end of the road which gives the easiest access to the Caldera. From near the town of El Paso, off the Santa Cruz de La Palma to Los Llanos road, a side road leads up to an interesting lookout known as **La Cumbrecita**. Nearby are two magnificent sites from which one can view the vast crater.

Both the **Mirador los Roques** and the **Mirador las Chozas** give the visitor some of the best views across the deep crater. Directly in front of the lookouts is an interesting rock pinnacle known as the **Roque de Idafe**. This spire was once worshipped by Guanche natives in pre-Columbian times and was the site of human sacrifices. Right across the other side of the crater, you'll be able to see the sharp outline of the Roques de los Muchachos and if the weather is clear you can make out the dome of the Observatory perched on the crater rim.

> **INSECT-COLOURED SILK**
>
> The small village of El Paso, near the road to La Cumbrecita, is renowned for its handmade silk, the only place in Spain where it is produced traditionally. A natural dye was first used in the 18th century to colour the silk. This was extracted from a lichen called *orchillo*, found on coastal rocks. In the early 19th century, a bug, which lives on the *optunia* (prickly pear), was introduced. When crushed, the bug produced a deep carmine dye, which was employed to colour the natural silk. Almond shells, when processed, were also used to give the silk a beige hue. In El Paso today, these three natural dyes are still used to produce vividly coloured silk items snapped up as souvenirs by tourists.

Below: *Breathtaking view from the Roque de los Muchachos into the Taburiente crater.*

Inside the huge crater is a wonderful fertile valley packed with colourful and unusual shrubs, trees and flowers, aided by frequent rain and damp, cool clouds. At certain heights, various types of vegetation thrive. From 1300m (4265ft) an unusual type of tree heather, *Erica arborea*, and the faya tree (*Myrica faya*) exist side by side. The faya is culled by locals as it is ideally suited for use as props for banana plants, grown on the terraces in the west of the island. From 1000m (3300ft) the **Canary Pine forest** extends up to almost 2000m (6200ft). This pine is unusual because it has the ability to withstand the forest fires which occasionally rage through La Palma's wooded areas. Unique to the Canaries is the 4m (13ft) high, biennial pininana flower. This unusual plant blooms blue on La Palma and red on Tenerife. La Palma violets also thrive in the caldera, as does the yellow-flowered cordeso and the pink and white cistus. Laurisilva, another of the Canarys' rare species of tree, which is not a real laurel, also proliferates at a certain level on the crater rim's slopes.

Returning to the island's north road, turn right and take a detour to the clifftop village of **Santa Domingo de Garafia** for views of the rocky coast and to see the fine church. There is a secret fountain near the crossroads at **Llano Negro** and the **Cueva de la Zarza** is the site of many Guanche rock inscriptions.

Passing the turning left to **Franceses**, to the right of the main road is **Roque Faro**, a goat-rearing centre. After **Barlovento** village, the road heads down to the junction with a road leading to the **Punta Cumplida** lighthouse, with fine coast vistas. Continue on the main road to **Los Sauces**, site of the 16th-century **Nuestra Señora de Monserrat** church which contains a 17th-century statue of the Virgin and a Flemish-style altarpiece. If you make a detour to the coastal village of **San Andrés y Sauces**, near the Barranco de Agua, you'll come across the picturesque fishing port of **Espindola**. Also near San Andrés is **El Charco Azul**, the Blue Pool.

THE DRAGON TREE

Dracaena draco, the dragon tree, sprouts like a giant mushroom in gardens and in the wilds of most of the Canary Islands. Said to be descended from a prehistoric type of vegetation, this strange tree, with its gnarled trunk and spiky, clustered leaves, certainly grows to a very old age, but its lack of rings means that it is impossible to date accurately. In ancient times, the Guanches used the resin as an ingredient for embalming their chiefs. They also used it to dye their garments. Dragon trees are now protected by government decree, and there are many fine specimens throughout the islands.

Bosque de los Tilos ★★★

The main road leads through deep gorges and, before the Barranco Galga lookout at San Bartolomé, the **Bosque de los Tilos**, a UNESCO-protected forest, is beautiful and well worth a visit. Halfway between here and Santa Cruz is the pretty town of **Puntallana**.

The south of the island vies with the north for natural beauty and the road which should be taken out of Santa Cruz leads up past the **Mirador El Risco**, or **Mirador de la Concepción**, through to Brena Alta which is famous for its palm weaving. There is a tobacco factory where you can buy good samples as souvenirs, and then you will pass two impressive dragon trees, and make you way down to **Breña Baja**. The International Airport is located south of here. Take the main, coastal road and look for the **Cueva de Belmaco** with its Guanche rock inscriptions.

MIRADORS ON THE ISLAND

- Pico de las Nieves: 2247m (7372ft).
- Panorama La Cumbrecita: 1633m (5357ft).
- Vulcán de San Antonio: 657m (2155ft).
- Mirador El Time: 594m (1948ft).
- Roque de los Muchachos: 2426m (7959ft).

Mazo ★★

Take the top road to see the 16th-century statues of the Virgin in the church of **San Blas** in the charming village of Mazo. During the festival of Corpus Christi, from May to June, the villagers decorate Mazo with carpets of flowers and arches of greenery. The village is well-known for its pottery and it's worth paying a visit to **El Molino**, on the main road after Breña Baja, a craft school. You'll also be able to buy souvenirs like woven baskets and embroidered tablecloths from the workshop.

Continuing through the villages of Monte de Luna and Las Caletas, the main road enters **Fuencaliente**. Today the village is noted for its excellent Malvasia wine and almond biscuits. Nearby are two volcanoes: **San Antonio** and **Teneguia** (formed when San Antonio erupted in 1971).

Opposite: *Dragon trees are quite common in the wilds throughout the islands. Their blood-red sap was used in ancient Guanche rituals.*
Below: *Appreciate the natural beauty of Las Palma's extinct volcanoes by exploring on foot.*

> **GUANCHE ARTEFACTS**
>
> The **Cueva de Belmaco**, in southern La Palma, was the home of the last Guanche king of Tigalete and Tihuya, who was captured in 1492. There are mysterious spiral inscriptions on the cave walls similar to those discovered in the **Cueva de la Zarza**, in the north of the island. No-one is certain whether these drawings and engravings are a form of writing, or astronomical calculations. Some rare archaeological finds have also come from the Belmaco cave. You can see these in the **Museum of Natural History** in Santa Cruz.

Near the San Antonio volcano is the spectacular **Roque Teneguia**, a spire once revered by the native Guanches. The Teneguia volcano is particularly interesting as it has only recently erupted. You'll discover that the ground is still warm under your feet. Also, the views from here of the wild lava landscape are spectacular. From this lookout you can walk down to the two lighthouses on the rocky **Punta de Fuencaliente**. After visiting the two volcanoes, take a detour west off the main road to **Las Indias** on the coast for stunning views of the bays. Back on the route north, past **El Charco**, is **Las Manchas**, where you'll see the fine, black sand beach of Puerto de Naos.

Puerto de Naos ★★★

The beach can only be reached by driving north through **Los Llanos** and back down to the steep coast, clad with banana plantations. Puerto de Naos is the best beach on La Palma and is the west coast's largest resort, located 11km (7 miles) south of Tazacorte.

The road winds through **San Nicolas**, a village split in two because of the volcanic eruption of Nambroque, in 1949, which left the little church isolated among the lava fields. As you approach Los Llanos, you will drive through **Tajuya** village, around which the region becomes highly agricultural with fruit and almond orchards, profuse flower gardens and tobacco plantations.

> **SAFARIS**
>
> **Jeep Safaris** are a good way to get off the beaten track and explore terrain inaccessible to ordinary hire cars, but rattling around in the back of a rather uncomfortable four-wheel drive is not everyone's idea of fun. **Boat Safaris**, available from most of the larger tourist resorts, offer all sorts of trips around the islands. The most interesting ones leave from southern Tenerife in search of whales and dolphins. If you're feeling more energetic, you could go on a horse, donkey or camel safari. Children will love it.
> Tourist offices will be able to give you information on the types of excursions available.

Right: *The black sand beach of Puerto de Naos.*

La Palma at a Glance

BEST TIMES TO VISIT

Temperatures vary little on La Palma throughout the year, but there is plenty of rain from November to the end of March. The sea temperatures are consistant and one can swim all year round.

GETTING THERE

Most visitors from abroad, apart from those from the Spanish mainland, arrive by air at **La Palma International Airport**. There are **ferry services** from Cádiz for passengers and cars to Santa Cruz.

GETTING AROUND

La Palma has a good bus service but most people prefer to travel off the bus routes. This is why **car hire** is the best way to get around. Prices vary but mileage is usually unlimited. Organized **coach tours** take visitors to various island attractions. Coach excursions can be joined from pre-arranged pick-up points and can last for a half or full day.

WHERE TO STAY

Santa Cruz
LUXURY
Parador Nacional Santa Cruz, Avenida Maritima 34; tel: (922) 41 23 40, fax: 41 18 56; prestigious hotel in villa.

MID-RANGE
Hotel Maritimo, Avda. Maritimo 80; tel: (922) 42 02 22, fax: 41 43 02; good position on harbour.

Brena Baja
MID-RANGE
Hacienda San Jorge, Playa de los Cancajos; tel: (922) 18 10 66, fax: 43 45 28; Spanish-style hotel near small beach.

El Paso
BUDGET
Nambroque, Calle Montelujan; tel: (922) 48 52 79; well-located, great facilities.

Fuencaliente
BUDGET
Apartamentos Colón, Los Quemados; tel: (922) 44 41 55; views of vineyards and the sea.

WHERE TO EAT

Santa Cruz
Chipi Chipi, Juan Mayor 42; tel: (922) 41 10 24; excellent dishes with typical hot sauces. Closed Wednesday, Sunday.

El Paso
La Cascada, Carretera de la Cumbre; tel: (922) 48 57 27; good pork dishes with *gofio*.

Fuencaliente
Parrilla Junonia, Los Canarios, Carretera General 49; tel: (922) 44 40 21; fresh fish and meat.

Breña Baja
Casa Pancho, La Polvacera 283; tel: (922) 43 48 34; fresh fish, pork and rabbit dishes.

San Andrés y Sauces
Meson del Mar, Puerto Esindola; tel: (922) 45 03 05; best fish restaurant.

TOURS AND EXCURSIONS

Botanical Excursions: Avenida del Puente 18, No. 3B, Santa Cruz de La Palma; tel: (922) 41 55 32.
Visits to the Astrophysical Observatory (Roque de los Muchachos): Instituto de Astrofisica de Canarias; tel: (922) 40 55 00 or 41 15 52.
Sportsfishing Club: la Gaviota, Avenida del Puente 27, No 1 Santa Cruz; tel: (922) 42 02 41.
Mountaineering: Los Llanos de Aridane; tel: (922) 46 00 85.

USEFUL CONTACTS

Aeropuerto de la Palma, tel: (922) 44 61 00 or 41 15 40.
IBERIA Airlines, Real 30, Santa Cruz, tel: (922) 41 31 60.
Tourist Information Offices
Santa Cruz: Paseo Maratimo/Calle O'Daly, tel: (922) 41 19 57 or 41 21 06.
Puerto de la Cruz: Tourist Information Office, Plaza de la Iglesia 3, tel: (922) 38 60 00 or 37 02 43.
Travel Agents
Bandama: Avenida Maritima 20, Santa Cruz; tel: (922) 41 50 57, fax: 41 50 57.
Viajes Calima: Apuran 9, Santa Cruz; tel: (922) 42 00 04.
Viajes Insular: Plaza de España 2, Santa Cruz; tel: (922) 46 04 59.
Palmatur: Alvarez de Abreu 72, Santa Cruz; tel: (922) 42 04 94.
Omnibus service: tel: (922) 41 19 24 or 46 02 41.
Ferry service: Transmediterranea, tel: (922) 41 11 21.

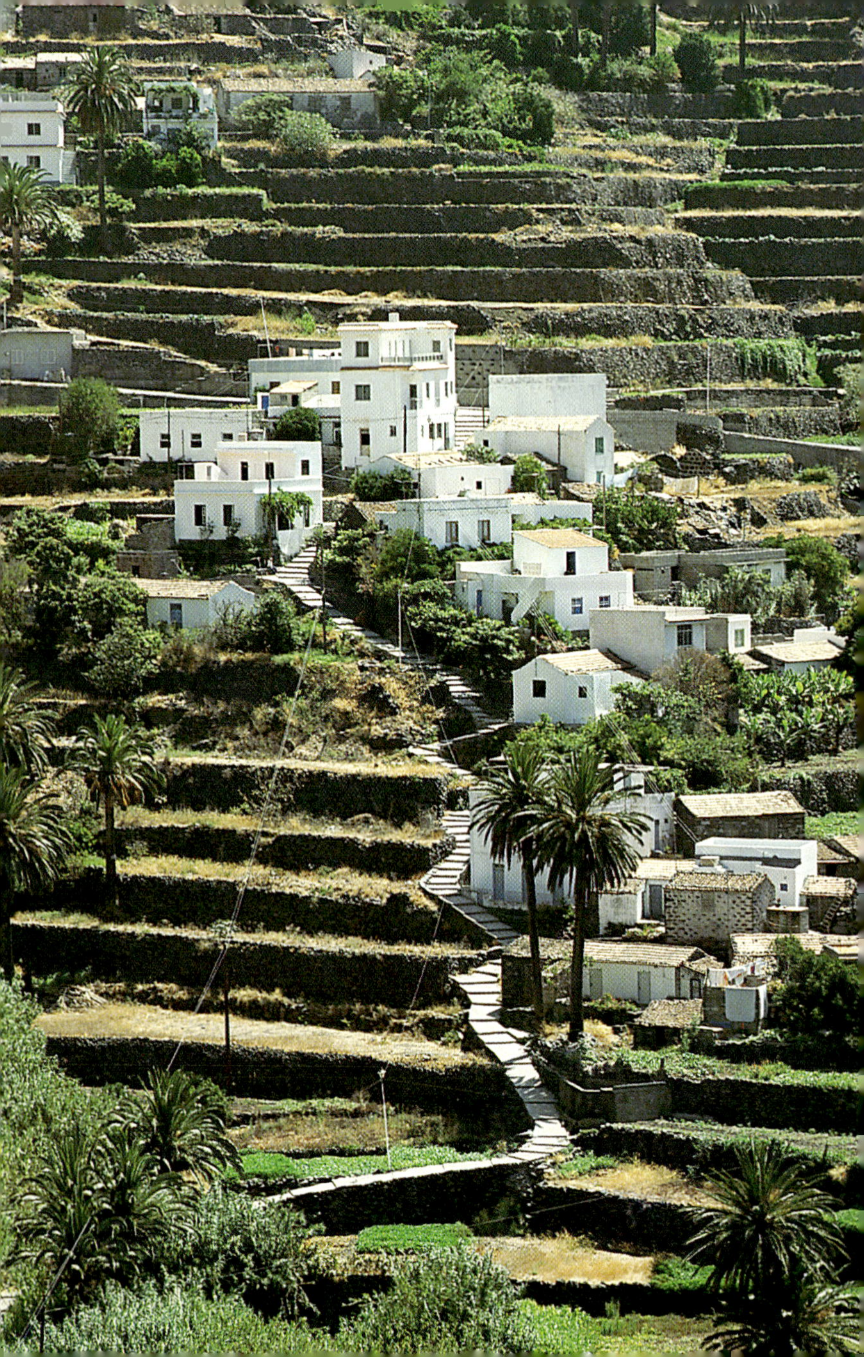

8
La Gomera and El Hierro

Almost circular in shape, with the **National Park of Garajonay** in its centre, **La Gomera** is an extinct volcano and is thoroughly unspoilt. Once inhabited by a proud branch of the Guanche race, this sixth largest island of the Canary archipelago is still comparatively wild, ringed by steep cliffs, crammed with high peaks and covered by lush foliage. About two-thirds of the 372km^2 (144 sq mile) island is forested, and it is dominated by the massif of **Garajonay**, rising to 1487m (4879ft), whose jagged spines radiate out towards the sea. There are six major *barrancos* (gorges) dividing the countryside.

An important natural feature is the vast cedar forest, the **Bosque del Cerdo**, not far from the capital, and mastic gum trees, pines, and moss-encrusted silver laurel abound in the numerous deep valleys, dating back millions of years. The forests of La Gomera have been declared a Natural Heritage of Mankind site by UNESCO, and are criss-crossed with tracks which are ideal for walkers.

El Hierro is the smallest and least known of all the Islands. Visitors who seek peace and quiet are drawn to this westerly island which offers wonderful walking opportunities. Superb pine forests, sheer mountain walls and fantastic lookout points or *miradores* are also available to the visitor. A great natural feature of El Hierro is the bay of **El Golfo** (the Gulf). Some believe this to be the rim of a large crater, half of which is sunken and the other rising theatrically to over 1000m (3281ft).

DON'T MISS

*** **Playa de Santiago:** stony beach overlooked by quaint fishing village.
*** **Valle Gran Rey:** called 'Valley of the Great King' with beautiful views of the valley. Enjoy the emerald-green slopes, pretty villages and La Playa Calera.
*** **Parque Nacional de Garajonay:** contains a woodland of ferns, laurels and heath trees. This *Laurasilva* forest offers popular walks.
*** **Vallehermoso:** features the spectacular Los Organos rock formations.
*** **Hermigua:** the island's richest banana-growing area.

Opposite: *Gomeran farmers plant crops on steep hillsides terraces.*

SIGHTS TO SEE

*** Christopher Columbus's House: the explorer's base on the island.
*** Torre de Conde: Pre-Columbian Americana Museum.
*** Pozzo de Aguada: well from which the expeditions drew their last water before sailing to the New World.
*** Church of The Assumption: links to Columbus and the Conquistador Cortez.

Right: *The dense forest of the Garajonay National Park dominates La Gomera and is a favourite spot for hiking.*

LA GOMERA

This island is often shrouded in cloud, and can only be reached by a 90-minute ferry trip or half-hour hydrofoil from **Los Cristianos** in Tenerife, as there is no commercial airport on the island. This isolation, and the lack of golden sandy beaches, keeps many would-be holidaymakers at arm's length. Visitors come here mainly for the fantastic and dramatic scenery and for its tranquil, laid-back atmosphere and way of life. Just under 18,000 people live here, many of whom show the typical features of their Guanche ancestors. Other Canarios are known to make jokes about the Gomerans and poke fun at the isolated islanders. Handfashioned pottery, dating from around

Above: *A typical Gomerian building at Hermigua, La Gomera.*

3000BC, has been found in the area of **Fortaleza** which is situated in the centre of the island. Similar pots, the ochre-coloured, beautifully glazed 'ollas', are still being made on the island today.

A Brief History

In the late 15th and early 16th centuries, **Christopher Columbus** and **Hernando Cortez** visited the island. This was Columbus's final port of call before his historic journey across the Atlantic in 1492. It's La Gomera's main claim to international fame. The island's other link with the New World is that many Gomerans emigrated to Venezuela. The tiny capital, **San Sebastián**, nestles in the folds of the sunny east coast, while the north coast receives a year-round buffeting from the rain-filled northeast trade winds. One main road rings the **National Park of Garajonay**, with spur roads or connections to the six major villages of Hermigua, Agulo, Vallehermoso, Valle Gran Rey, La Rajita and Playa de Santiago. The largest hotel, **Hotel Jardín Tecina**, is situated above Santiago beach and consists of a village of cabana-like, cliff-top bungalows.

CHRISTOPHER COLUMBUS IN GOMERA

It was no accident that Columbus chose to visit the tiny island of Gomera. He had heard that an old flame, whom he had first met in Granada, was living on Gomera. Her name was Dona Beatriz de Peraza y Bobadilla, Marquesa de Moya. She lived in a tower, the Torre del Conde, in San Sebastián.

On his first visit to the island, Columbus dallied with Beatriz for a few days, possibly delaying the discovery of the Americas! On each of his subsequent three voyages, Columbus made a point of visiting his tower-bound lover.

Above: *The natural harbour of San Sebastián, last port of call for Columbus before setting sail on his 1492 voyage of discovery.*

CANARIES

There is hardly anywhere on the Canary Islands where birds are not singing. The most celebrated bird is the island's canary, *Serinus canarius*. Almost every bar, café, restaurant and balcony has a woven cane birdcage containing one of these extraordinary singing birds. These cages containing a singing bird is endemic to the Canary Islands, Madeira and the Azores.

SAN SEBASTIAN DE LA GOMERA

A giant statue of Christ overlooks the island's capital. The statue's arm is outstretched towards the distant Americas. San Sebastián harbour is one of the finest natural harbours in the entire Canary Islands.Rather disappointing initially, a closer look at this town reveals some interesting architecture. Consisting mostly of box-like, whitewashed, modern buildings, this port has no highrise structures but does have a few pretty, Spanish Baroque and Moorish-style, pantiled houses built around shady courtyards. The Town Council building contains works by a local painter, José Aguilar. The city's main square and meeting place is **Plaza Calvo Sotelo**.

Christopher Columbus

The house at number 56 **Calle del Medio** is where Columbus stayed in San Sebastián, and is now a museum. Nearby is the well-house he used, known as the **Pozzo de Aguada**, which bears the legend 'With this Water, America was Baptized'. Columbus's ships, the *Santa María*, *Nina* and *Pinta*, arrived in San Sebastián on the explorer's first voyage to discover the New World in

1492. The three ships set sail from La Gomera, the last land they would set foot on before their arrival in the Americas. The next time Columbus arrived in La Gomera he came with a fleet of 17 ships on his second voyage west in October 1493. Again, in 1498 and in 1502, Columbus used the port as his final replenishing point before venturing out across the Atlantic Ocean.

Church of the Assumption **

Between the well-house and the house where Columbus stayed is the 15th-century **Church of the Assumption**, where the explorer heard his last mass before departing on his epic voyage. The exterior doorway has a remarkable lava-stone, Gothic central façade, and frescoes, created in 1760, which depict a fleet of English ships on the attack. A plaque on the wall records the worship of the Spanish conquistador, Hernando Cortez, in this church.

Torre del Conde ***

Currently a National Historic Monument, this Torre del Conde or Count's Tower dates back to 1447. This ancient tower is the oldest surviving military building in the Canaries. The Torre del Conde also contains an important museum of fascinating pre-Columbian Americana, celebrating the connection of the island with the vast continent around 6500km (4000 miles) to the west.

The tower was built in 1447 and it's the town's

Below: *Torre del Conde in San Sebastián is the oldest military building on the islands and was once home of Beatriz de Bobadilla, mistress of Columbus.*

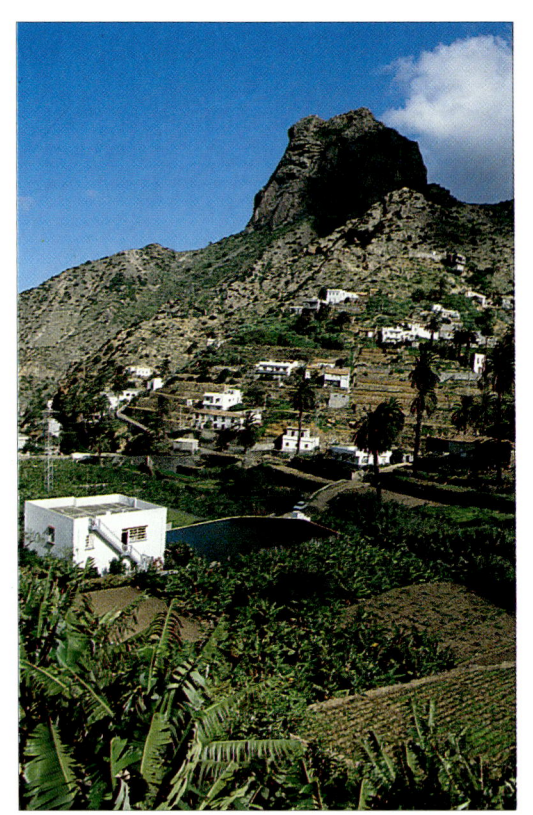

Above: *Los Organos, the spectacular basalt cliff near Vallehermoso, comprised hundreds of columns of rock.*

most striking monument. Beatriz de Bobadilla used it as a refuge after the slaying of her husband, Hernán Peraza in 1487. Today it is surrounded by a car park, with an odd palm tree standing out in relief.

El Hierro

This is the smallest of the Canary Islands, at only 277km^2 (106 sq miles). Approximately 7000 people live on El Hierro, which lies, like an inverted anvil, way out in the southwestern corner of the archipelago. This tranquil island is devoid of any form of commercialism and is packed with incredibly beautiful and rather dramatic scenery.

The people of El Hierro are the descendants of the ancient **Bimbache** tribes, who worshipped the sacred Garoe evergreen tree, which produced water from its leaves. In Roman times, the island was inhabited by giant lizards, a throwback to the prehistoric iguanas which once thrived here. In his *Natural History*, Pliny called Hierro, 'Lagartaria', or 'Land of the Lizards', and a few examples of these creatures exist to this day on the Roques de Salmor, off the northwest coast.

For thousands of years, until Columbus proved otherwise, El Hierro was considered the end of the world. The first zero meridian was originally measured from the old lighthouse on **Orchilla**, the island's westernmost tip. This was the last piece of land which

EL HIERRO 119

INTERESTING ALTERNATIVES

*** **El Golfo:** huge, crescent-shaped bay on the west coast, fantastic views.
** **Frontera:** the island's second settlement and famous wine region.
** **Sabinosa:** famous for spa spring waters; westernmost settlement.
** **Pozo de la Salud:** underwater fishing attraction.
** **El Tamaduste:** a natural pool of remarkably clear water
** **Tinor:** spectacular formations of volcanic ash amid bright green fields.

Columbus was to see until he landed in the Bahamas in 1492. Today, the main occupation on the island is cultivating the rich volcanic soil and raising cattle. Minor roads link several beauty spots and hamlets, as well as the island's Parador, one of only two hotels on El Hierro.

Below: *The ferry for El Hierro leaves from the picturesque village of Santiago on La Gomera.*

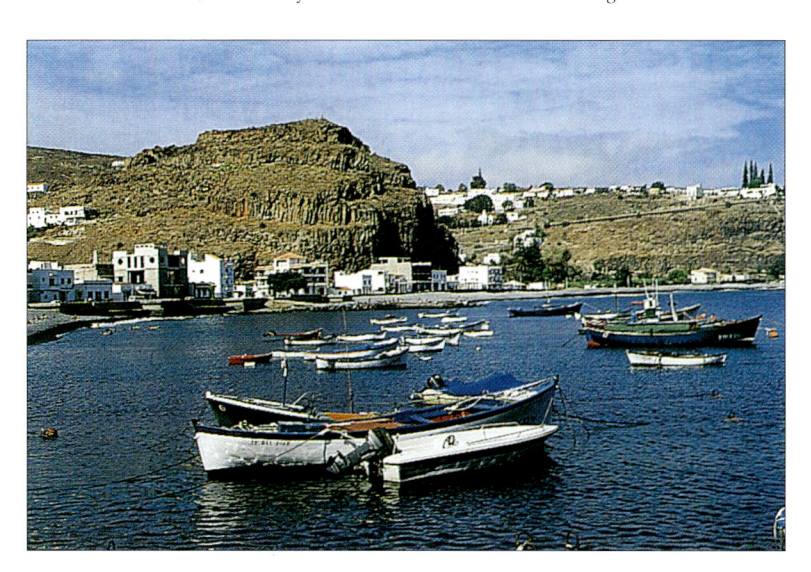

BEST BEACHES

There are 35 beaches on the island, with the best located on the east-facing coast. The longest beach, more than 3km (2 miles) in length, is the stretch of sand including the Playas Almorranas, Playecillas, Arena, the Playa de los Cardones and the Playa de las Calcosas, fronting the El Hierro Parador.

Below: *Herreño fishermen: fresh fish caught in the deep Atlantic Ocean are a staple ingredient of the Canarian diet.*

Valverde **

With exactly half of the island's inhabitants living in the capital, Valverde is a quiet, tranquil town with beautiful gardens, orchards, squares and a fine central plaza. The parish church is worth a visit, as are the town's market and fish restaurants. Unusually for the Canary Islands, this capital lies around 5km (3 miles) inland from the port of El Puerto de la Estaca, and a little less from the island's airport, both located on the east coast. The island's only state-run Parador is located at the end of a 14km (9 mile) coastal road which runs along the base of the sheer mountain wall of El Risco de los Herrenos, to the south of Valverde.

El Golfo ***

The large, 14km (9 mile) long, crescent-shaped bay of El Golfo in the west of the island was once part of a giant volcano rim, and it is the only place that the steep cliffs which surround the entire island, give way to a sloping shoreline. Its terraces, and El Golfo Valley, are ideal for growing paw paw, bananas, avocados, almonds, figs and vines.

This is the best point from which to see the bay. The high plateau in the centre of the island rises to 1501m (4295ft) at **Malpaso Point**. Volcanic craters dot the island's interior, a fertile area which supports trees that are hundreds of years old. **Frontera village,** almost in the centre of the island, is located in a good wine-producing region.

La Gomera and El Hierro at a Glance

BEST TIMES TO VISIT

The weather here is fine throughout the year. The northern side of the island, as well as the mountain forests can be quite damp. The islands of La Graciosa, Montaña Clara and Alegranza are generally hotter than El Hierro due to their close aspect to the African coast.

GETTING THERE

The best way to get to La Gomera is by **ferry** from Los Cristianos in the south of Tenerife to San Sebastián on La Gomera. Both a subsidiary of the Fred Olsen Line and Compania Transmediterranea run ferry services. El Hierro is reached from La Palma by **plane**. To get to the other smaller islands it's much easier to hire a **boat**.

GETTING AROUND

The **bus service** is less reliable on La Gomera than on the larger islands. A **hire car** is best to get around the island.

WHERE TO STAY

La Gomera
LUXURY
Parador Nacional Conde de La Gomera, San Sebastián; tel: (922) 87 11 00; good restaurant.

MID-RANGE
Garajonay, Calle Ruz de Padron 15, San Sebastián; tel: (922) 87 05 50; limited facilities, but central.

El Hierro
LUXURY
Parador del Hierro, Las Playas 26; tel: (922) 55 80 36, fax: 55 80 86; welcoming and well-furnished.

MID-RANGE
Boomerang, Calle Dr Gost 1, Valverde, El Hierro; tel: (922) 55 02 00, fax: 55 02 53; situated in town, friendly and comfortable.
Punta Grande Hotel, Las Puntas, Frontera, El Hierro; tel: (922) 55 90 81; quaintly listed as the smallest hotel in the world, classed as a two-star hotel it has marvellous views and a good restaurant.

BUDGET
Casanas, San Francisco 9; tel/fax: (922) 55 02 54; friendly and cheap.

WHERE TO EAT

La Gomera
Casa del Mar, Avenida Fred Olsen 61, San Sebastián, La Gomera; tel: (922) 87 12 19; fronting the beach with *pargo* fish and *ternera*, a speciality. Closed Sundays.
Mirador del Palmarejo, Carretera Gral. de Arure, 38870, Valle Gran Rey; La Gomera; tel: (922) 80 58 68; regional food is prepared by students of gastronomy.
La Romantica, Boulevard La Oliva, s/n; tel: (922) 80 07 41; roast chicken and pizza a speciality.

El Hierro
Casa Juan, Valverde, El Hierro; tel: (922) 55 80 02; tempting seafood, worth sampling.
Punta Grande Hotel, Las Puntas-Frantera, El Hierro; tel: (922) 55 90 81; fax: 55 90 81; four rooms, school restaurant. Closed Monday and Tuesday.

TOURS AND EXCURSIONS

The **C.I.T.** (Centro de Iniciatives y Tourismo del Norte de La Gomera) organize guided tours, tel and fax: (922) 14 41 01.
The Juego de Bolas Visitor's Centre of Garajonay National Park (UNESCO and ICONA) organize tours. Park Offices: San Sebastián, La Gomera; tel: (922) 80 09 93.
Los Organos: excursions by boat from Valle Gran Rey, Playa de Santiago and other ports on La Gomera.
El Golfo: best to visit the west side of this island.
El Pinar: in the centre of El Hierro, a forest of Canarian pines with numerous lookouts.

USEFUL CONTACTS

Tourist Board, Cabildo Insular del Hierro, Valverde; tel: (922) 14 01 47.
Patronado de Turismo, Licenciado Bueno 1, Valverde; tel: (922) 55 03 02.
Aeropuerto de Hierro Valverde; tel: (922) 44 01 15.
Tourist Information Office, Dr. Quintero 11, Valverde; tel: (922) 14 01 47.
Autos Cruz Alta Car Hire, Valverde, tel: (922) 55 03 49.

Travel Tips

Tourist Information
The **Spanish Tourist Office** maintains offices in France (Paris), Italy (Milan), Germany (Munich), America (New York), Australia (Sydney) and Canada (Toronto). The **Spanish Tourist Office** has its headquarters in London at 57-58 St James Street London SW 1A 1LD; tel: (171) 499 1169, fax: (171) 629 42 57.
Local Island Tourist Boards offer general advice, sell tickets, rent cars and offer trips and other services but may not speak much English. You will find them all over the islands and in the major resorts; the main ones are as follows:
Fuerteventura, Avenida 1st May 39, Puerto del Rosario. tel: (928) 85 14 00, fax: 85 18 12.
Lanzarote, Parque José Ramírez Cerda; tel/fax: (928) 81 18 60.
Tenerife, Cabildo Insular de Tenerife, Palacio Insular, Plaza de España, Santa Cruz; tel: (922) 24 22 27, fax:60 57 81.
La Palma, Calle O'Daly 22, Santa Cruz; tel: (922) 41 16 41 or 41 19 57 or 41 21 06.
La Gomera, Calle Medio 4, San Sebastian; tel: (922) 14 01 47 or 87 01 55 or 14 01 51.
El Hierro, Cabildo Insular del Hiero, Valverde; tel: (922) 55 03 02, fax: 55 10 52.
Visit the Canary Islands website: www.gobcan.es

Entry Requirements
No visa is required, but visitors must have a valid passport. British, Australian, Canadian, New Zealand and American visitors can stay for up to three months. Those staying longer require visas, and workers need a special permit. If you lose your passport, contact the consul of the country of issue and they will advise you how to obtain the necessary documentation.

Customs
The Canary Islands are a **free-trade zone** and there are no restrictions on what you may bring with you as a tourist. The amount of wine, spirits, tobacco and other goods that can be taken in and out of the Canary Islands depends on whether you are travelling to or from an EU country, a non-EU country or a country outside Europe. Visitors should check in their country of residence before travelling abroad.

Health Requirements
No special vaccinations are required except for those visiting from endemic smallpox, cholera or yellow fever zones. **Typhoid** and **paratyphoid vaccinations** are recommended by British Health Authorities. Nationals of EU countries, including British visitors, can obtain a certain degree of free medical care with an **E111 form**, but medicines or dental treatment must be paid for. Take your E111 form to a local Instituto de la Seguridad Social (**Social Security Office**) when you have had medical treatment. Health insurance is recommended, and keep all receipts for treatment, in the event that you need to make a claim.

Getting There
By Air: There are regular cheap charter flights direct to Gran Canaria, Lanzarote, Fuerteventura and Tenerife from most western European cities. Scheduled flights are expensive and go via Madrid.
By Boat: Ferries from Cádiz on mainland Spain connect with Las Palmas on Gran

Canaria, Arrecife on Lanzarote and Santa Cruz on Tenerife. The ferry or hydrofoil from Los Cristianos on Tenerife runs to San Sebastián on Gomera.

What To Pack

The golden rule is to travel light whenever possible. There are several essentials to consider.

For women a shawl is useful because it can double up as a beach wrap, a head covering for church visits or as an evening wrap when a sudden drop in temperature could make you feel quite chilly. Men are advised to take a light jacket for the same reason. Dress as though you were in the tropics, with cotton shirts and trousers, light skirts or jeans, T-shirts, shorts (not recommended for church and business meetings), swimming costumes, a sarong and smart clothes for dining out. Take comfortable walking shoes, a pair of smarter shoes, at least one pair of sandals or 'flip-flops', sunglasses and a hat.

Should you forget something vital, local shops, especially those in resorts, sell most items of clothing ranging from the locally-made (which can be elegant and fashionable) to the designer labels. Canarians themselves usually dress casually.

Money Matters

Currency: The Spanish peseta (pta) is used throughout the islands and comes in notes of 1000, 2000, 5000 and 10,000ptas. Coins come in denominations of 5, 10, 25, 50, 100, 200 and 500ptas.

Currency exchange: You can change foreign currency or travellers' cheques at banks, post offices, bureaux de change and many hotels.

Banks: There are numerous banks throughout the islands, open on weekdays from 09:00–14:00 and Saturdays from 09:00–13:00. Banks will exchange Eurocheques free but will usually charge for exchanging travellers' cheques or currency. You will need your passport when changing money or travellers' cheques.

Credit cards: All major credit cards are accepted throughout the islands in banks, the larger hotels, travel agents and exchange offices.

Tipping: Tipping is not obligatory in the Canaries as a service charge is generally added to hotel and restaurant bills. Porters, hotel staff, taxi drivers and guides, however, will expect a small gratuity. Known on the islands as a *propina*, a small tip is also expected by waiters in restaurants and it is usual to leave a few coins after having a drink and tapas at a bar.

A service charge is generally added to food bills, but it is customary to leave some small change, between 5–10% of the bill.

Accommodation

Most resorts throughout the islands have a range of hotels from super-luxury with all facilities to pensions which are full-board only. Hotels are categorized from five stars for luxury hotels, through modest hotels (hostales) to pensions or hostels, which are classed as one-star. Aparthotels often have the usual facilities but there are also self-catering rooms which have cooking facilities. Hotels described as *residencias* have no restaurant, but often serve breakfast. The state-run Paradores, located on each island, are generally located in fine mansions, or in places of interest to tourists. Gran Canaria and Tenerife have official camping sites but there is no objection at all to camping anywhere on the islands except in the National Parks.

Eating Out

Most towns and cities have a wide range of restaurants, bistros and cafés, catering to a wide variety of international or local tastes, as do the resort areas. Eating places inland on the islands, or away from villages, are not so common and, away from tourist areas, will concentrate on local cuisine. Lunch generally starts from 14:00 and evening dinner from 20:00. Fish restaurants are common-place and good value for money, as is most food in the Canaries. There are a few designated picnic sites known as *zonas recreativas*.

Transport

Air: Inter-island flights connect airports on every island except La Gomera.

Ferries: Every island is served by regular ferry services mostly run by Compania Transmediterranea.

Buses: There are fast, cheap, regular bus services on Gran Canaria and Tenerife. Those on the other islands are less reliable and hitch-hiking is commonplace. For a 40% discount on cash bus fares, buy a 'bond' ticket from the local tourist office, otherwise buy your ticket on board.

Car Hire: In theory you must have an International Driving Licence if driving in the Canaries or renting a car but in practice valid driver's licences are accepted.

Taxis: Taxis are metered, but there are set-rates for long distances and tours.

Road Rules: In the Canary Islands you drive on the right, overtake on the left and give right of way to traffic coming from the right. Seatbelts must be worn at all times and children under the age of ten must travel in the back of the car. Always carry your driving licence. As the police can demand to see your passport at any time, it is a good idea to carry photocopies of the relevant pages around with you. By law you must carry a set of spare bulbs for your headlamps and rear lights and a regulation warning triangle.

If you take your own car to the islands you will need an International Driving Licence, car registration papers, a nationality sticker, a red warning triangle, a Green Card extension to your insurance policy and a bail bond. Speed limits are 120kph (75mph) on motorways; 100kph (70mph) on dual carriageways; 90kph (55mph) on other roads, but 60kph (35mph) in built-up areas. Seat belts must be worn on all roads outside built-up areas. Roads vary from multi-lane motorways to dirt tracks in rural areas, where you are likely to encounter donkeys and carts. The main cities can be quite congested.

Driving hints: Overheating in hot weather is a common problem so check the water level in the radiator regularly. If your engine has run dry, let it cool down before topping up with water or you will cause severe engine damage. If the radiator is overheating, allow the water in it to cool first before attempting to remove the radiator cap.

Petrol can vaporize in the fuel lines, fuel pump or carburettor, during the prolonged ascents or in high temperatures. Should this happen, let the engine cool down (a damp cloth over the engine will speed up the process).

Take spare water and oil on journeys, check you've the necessary documents and accessories and carry enough money to pay for on the spot fines (for parking offences, traffic violations, etc). Avoid drinking and driving.

Breakdowns and Accidents
In the event of a breakdown, it is illegal to tow one car behind another. Minor accidents are not generally reported to the police. A car may be impounded by the police after any serious accident until the legalities have been completed. Whatever the accident, car registration details, names and addresses are best exchanged and, if the car is hired, report any incident to the hire firm and insurance company.

ROAD SIGNS

alquilar • to hire
alto • stop
altopista • highway
camino cerrado • road closed
ceda el paso • give way
camion • lorry
carro • car
circamvalacion • bypass
cruce • crossroads
cuidado • warning
curva peligrosa • dangerous bend
derecha • right
derecho • straight on
direccion unica • one-way
gasolina • petrol
goma • tyre
izquierda • left
no adelantar • no overtaking
no parquero • no parking
pare • stop
parquero • car park
petroleo • petrol
ponchera • puncture
reduzca velocidad • reduce speed
salida departure • exit
semaforo • traffic lights
servicentro • services

Maps: Good road maps of the Canary Islands are available in most European languages. There are many detailed maps of the larger towns and cities. The best source for maps of the islands are the Spanish Tourist Offices. Bookshops throughout the islands sell maps, including useful street maps. Local tourist information centres will provide you with free guide pamphlets and information leaflets. Also available in this series is the *Globetrotter Travel Map of the Canary Islands* (New Holland).

Business Hours

Most offices, whether they are government or commercial (including the shops), are open from 09:00–13:00 and 15:00–19:00 on weekdays, 09:00–13:00 on Saturdays.

Time Difference

The Canary Islands keep to Greenwich Mean Time in winter and so maintain a one-hour difference with Continental Time. The clocks go back one hour in summer.

Communications

Telephones: The Canary Islands are divided into two for administrative purposes, and so the telephone codes vary from island to island. Gran Canaria, Fuerteventura and Lanzarote have the prefix 928. Tenerife, La Palma, La Gomera and El Hierro are prefixed 922. The area code now should be dialled as part of the telephone or fax number. Police emergency number is **091** or **092**. Ambulance **061**.
Post: When posting mail to an address in the Canaries write your name and address on the back of the envelope or package together with the word *remitente*.

The postal service is rather slow and laid back. Stamps (*sellos* or *timbres*) can be purchased from Post Offices (*correos*) and from many postcard shops, tobacconists, hotels and some bars. Post boxes are painted yellow. Any urgent mail should be sent either with a reliable traveller or by one of the international courier companies.

Electricity

Most tourist hotels are serviced by a 100 volt system, but 220–240 volts is the norm throughout the islands. A two-pin (round) electric adaptor is recommended for travelling to the islands.

Weights and Measurements

The metric system is in use throughout the islands.

Health Services

Citizens of EU countries are entitled to free medical treatment (except dental), and, for UK visitors, an E111 Form should be obtained before travelling. This should be presented to the office in most cases. In the event of **illness and injury** there are hospitals in all major towns as well as many privately run medical clinics throughout the islands. Chemists or *farmacias* display a green cross outside their shops and at least one per town will stay open all night. Notices of which pharmacists are on duty are posted in the chemists windows and in local newspapers.

USEFUL PHRASES

Desayuno
• Breakfast
Comida
(de Mediodia) • Lunch
Cena • Dinner
Cuanto vale?
• How much is it?
Si • Yes
Non • No
Buenas dias
• Good morning
Buenos tardes
• Good afternoon
Buenos noches
• Good night
De nada
• You're welcome
Adios • Goodbye
Bien venido • Welcome
Por favor • Please
Gracias • Thank you
Bueno • Good
Propina • Tip
Aeropuerto • Airport
Cerrado • Closed
Abierto • Open
Officina de Correos
• Post Office
Farmacia • Chemist
Finca • Farm
Calle • Street
Ciudad • Town
Gasolina • Petrol

Good Reading

- Cioranescue, Alejandro (1980) *La Canarien, the text of Gadifer de la Salle and Jean de Béthancourt*. Tenerife.
- Dicks, Brian (1988) *Lanzarote, Fire Island*. Dryad, London.
- Glas, George (1764) *History of the Canary Islands*. From the Spanish
- Goulding, John and Margaret (1989) *Lanzarote Windrush*. Lanzarote, Island Guides, Gloucestershire.
- Fernanadez-Armesto (1982) *The Canary Islands after the Conquest*. Clarendon, Oxford.
- Mercer, John (1980) *The Canary Islanders*. Collins, London.
- Stone, Olivia (1887) *Tenerife and its Six Satellites*. Marcus Ward, London.

For the **disabled traveller** there are several tour operators which offer interesting holidays in the Canary Islands. Generally, provision for disabled travellers is poor. Most monuments are not accessible either due to their location, or because of the numerous steps. Public transport is not very well-equipped or prepared for the disabled, nor are most toilet facilities, telephones or any other public facility. The authorities and hotel companies, however, are becoming more aware of the needs of disabled travellers and are gradually adapting their services in order to accommodate them.

Health Precautions

The most common ailments visitors require treatment for are **sunburn** and **dehydration**. Salt pills and quantities of non-alcoholic liquids diminish the effects of too much sun. The sun is at its strongest 11:00–15:00 and you are advised to wear a wide-brimmed hat during the summer. Use a good, expensive sun block. Nausea, lethargy, increased heart beat, headaches and cramps are signs of sunstroke. Take a rehydration solution (sugar, salt and water) and get medical attention. Sunglasses are a must in the hot Canary Islands sun.

Although water is fine for drinking, it is advisable rather to use bottled water outside the tourist resorts. *Agua sin gas* is still water, and *agua con gas* is fizzy water.

Malaria is not a problem on the Islands, but mosquitoes are prevalent and an insect repellant is useful. Cover up well and this is especially applicable in the evenings.

Emergencies

In the case of **emergencies**, it is advisable to call the **police**, tel: **091**. To call the **ambulance** in Gran Canaria Province, tel: (922) 24 59 21. In Tenerife Province, tel: (922) 28 18 00, or **061**.

Public Holidays and Festivals

Fiestas celebrate saints' days and religious occasions, and are usually held between June and September. Each island has several, the traditions and performances of which vary and include rituals which have survived for centuries.

Colourful firework displays, lively horse parades, fiery bonfires, parades of religious icons and traditional folk-dancing and rituals accompany fiestas which often mix pagan customs and religious elements. This is because the islanders have a long-standing dependency on nature, relying on agriculture and the fruits of the sea. Carnivals generally do not have any religious significance, being purely social events for the local community to enjoy.

Ferias or town fairs are often held in conjunction with the festive and very popular local carnival.

There are many local **public holidays** in the Canary Islands. There are also movable fiestas such as **Maunday Thursday** (Jueves Santo), **Good Friday** (Viernes Santo), **Easter** (Pascua), **Easter Monday** (Lunes de Pascua), and **Corpus Christi**, which can fall in May or July.

INDEX

accommodation 38–39, 50, 51, 64–65, 80–81, 96, 97, 111, 121, 122–126
Aguapark Octopus 95
Aguila Canyon 44
Angustias Gorge 104
Arrecife **69**
Atlantic Ocean 5, 6, 7

beaches
  Fuerteventura
    Playa de las Pillas 62
    Playa del Perchel 58
    Playa del Moro 58
    Playa Puerto Rico 61
    Playa de Barlovento de Jandia 63
    Playa de Cofete 63
    Playa de Corralejo 58
  Gran Canaria
    Playa del Inglés 85
    Canteras 42
  La Graciosa
    Playa Lambra 79
    Playa Francesa 79
    Playa Lambra 79
  Lanzarote
    Playa Honda 71
    Playa Blanca 71
    Guacineta 71
  Las Palmas
    Playa de las Canteras 31, 37
  Tenerife
    Playa de la Arena **16**
Betancuria 55, **59**
Bimbache tribes 118
Bishop's Palace, Tenerife 89
birds
  blue chaffinch 9
  canary 9
  canarian buzzard 9
  canarian oyster catcher 9
  chat 9
  Fuerteventuran houbara 9
  laurel pigeon 9
  toucan **9**
Caldera de Taburiente **6**, 99, 103
Carnaval **18**, **19**
Carthaginians 10, 31
Castles
  Fuerteventura
    Castillo de Fustes 59
    El Tostón 55

Gran Canaria
  Cabañas Palace 102
  Castillo de Santa Catalina 121
  Salazar Palace 102
Lanzarote
  Palace of Queen Ico 75
Las Palmas
  Castillo de la Luz 37
Tenerife
  La Nava 89
  San Miguel 94
Cathedrals *see* Churches
Caves
  Gran Canaria
    Cave of the Crosses 45
    Cuevas Blancas 49
    Del Pinar 49
    Painted Cave 45
  La Palma
    Cueva Bonita 104
    Cueva de Balmaco 109, 110
    Cueva de la Zarza 110
  Lanzarote
    Cueva de los Verdes 77
  Tenerife
    Cueva del Hielo 92
César Manrique 26, 67, 70, 71, 72, 76, 77
  mural **25**
  museum **70**
Churches
  Fuerteventura
    Iglesia Santa Maria de Betancuria 60
    Iglesia de la Virgen de la Regla 60
    Nuestra Señora de Candelaria 56
    Santa Maria Cathedral 54
  Gran Canaria
    Nuestra Señora del Pino 19, 46
    Santa Ana Cathedral 19, 33
  La Gomera
    Church of the Assumption 117
    Nuestra Señora de la Ascunción 19
  La Palma
    Nuestra Señora de Monserrat Church 108
    San Salvador 102
  Cliffs of the Giants 88
  Lanzarote
    Nuestra Señora de Guadeloupe 19, 76

San Gines Church 71
Las Palmas
  San Francisco 35
  San Telmo 35
  Santa Ana Cathedral 26
Tenerife
  Basilica of Candelaria 95
  Church of San Francisco 87
  Iglesia Nuestra Señora de la Concepción 87, 89
  La Concepción 90
  Pilar Church 87
  San Francisco Church 87
  Santa Iglesia Cathedral 89
  Santa Ana Church 94
Columbus, Christopher 11, **12**, 31, 35, 101, 114, 116, 119
Corralejo **57**, **58**
Cruz de Tejeda **47**

De Bobadilla, Beatriz 117, 118
De Béthancourt, Jean 11, 54, 54, 59, 69, 75, 79
dragon tree 8, 45, 89, 93, **108**, **109**
Drake, Francis 101

el silbo 18
El Golfo bay 5, 113, 120
El Hierro 5, 6, 7, 112–121
El Rio 58, 77
El Tigre 87
Euphorbia plant **8**

Festivals
  Fuerteventura
    Fiesta de la Virgen de Rosario 56
  Lanzarote
    Fiesta de La Virgen de los Volcanes 77
    San Gines Festival 21
  Gran Canaria
    La Virgen de Pinto Festival 21
    Nuestra Señora de la Luz Festival 21
    Virgen de las Nieves 21
  La Palma
    Nuestra Señora de Las Nieves 103, **104**
  El Hierro
    Nuestra Señora de las Nieves 21

Tenerife
  Opera Festival 21
  San Agustin Festival 21
  San Benito Abad 21
  San Isidro Labrador 21
  San Roque Festival 21
folk dancing 19, **28**
Foreign Legion **55**
Forests
  Tenerife
    La Esperanza Forest 92
    Las Mercedes Forest 90
  La Gomera
    Bosque del Cerdo 113
  La Palma
    Bosque de los Tilos 109
Franco, General 11, 14, 15, 35, 63, 92
Fuerteventura 5, 6, 7, 52–65

Gando Airport 41, 79
Garachico 83, 88, 93, **94**
Gardens
  Lanzarote
    Jardin de Cactus **76**
  Tenerife
    Botanical Gardens of Acclimatization **91**
    Jardin Garcia Sanabria 87
gofio 23, 61
Gran Canaria 5, 7, 40–51
Guanches 8, **10**, 45

Hermitages
  Gran Canaria
    Hermitage of Cueva de la Virgen 48
    Hermitage of San Pedro 46
    Hermitage of Saint Isidro de Viejo 45
    Hermitage of La Virgen de Las Nieves 45
  Fuerteventura
    Las Mercedes Hermitage 56
    Hermitage of San Francisco 59
  Lanzarote
    Hermitage de la Virgen de los Dolores 77
  Las Palmas
    Hermitage of San Antonio Abad 35
  Tenerife
    Hermitage of El Calvario 90
Herreño fishermen **120**

INDEX

House museums
  Fuerteventura
    Casa del Capellan 56
    Casa de las Salinas 59
    Casa de los Coroneles 55, 56, 57
  Las Palmas
    Casa de Colón 26, 31, 34
International Astrophysical Observatory 106
Isla Graciosa **79**

Jandía Peninsula **53**, 61, **62**

La Geria 72, 73, **75**
La Gomera 5, 7, 112–121
La Graciosa 79
La Haria **77**, **78**
La Laguna 83, 88, 89
La Orotava 83, 88, 90
La Oliva 56
La Palma 5, 6, 7, 98–111
Lanzarote 5, 6, 7, 58,66–81
Las Palmas 30–39, 41
Las Teresitas 83, **90**
Los Llanos 99, 104, 110
Los Organos **118**
Los Rodeos Airport 89

Malmsey wine 9, 67, 87
Malocello, Lanzarotto 10, 68
Malpais **72**
Mardi Gras **20**
Maspalomas 58, 94
Miradors (viewpoints)
  Gran Canaria
    Finger of God 45
    La Silla mirador 48
    Pico de Bandama 46
    Posador mirador 49
  La Palma
    La Concepción 103
    Las Chozas mirador 107
    Los Roques 107
  Tenerife
    Margarita Diedra 93
    Pico del Inglés 90
    Punta de la Rasca 83
    Valley of Ariba 93
Mountains
  Lanzarote
    Montaña Amarilla 78
    Montaña Bermeja 78
    Montaña Clara 78
    Montaña del Fuego 71
    Montaña Guardilama 74
    Montaña de Mojón 79

Fuerteventura
  Devil's Claw 56
  Jandía Mountain 63
  Montaña Quemada 56
Gran Canaria
  Montaña de Cuatro Puertas 43
  Montaña del Gallego 43
La Graciosa
  Montaña Bermeja 79
Tenerife
  Anaga Mountains 83, 84, 89
  Mount Teide 5, **6**, 7, 8, 48, 83, **92**
Moorish architecture **28**
Museums
  Tenerife
    Aimeyda Military Museum 87
    Archaeological and Anthropological Museum 85
    Fine Arts Museum 86
    Museo de Artesania Ibero Americana 90
    Museum of Natural Science 87
  Fuerteventura
    Archaeological Museum 60
  Lanzarote
    Casade Carta Ethnological Museum 26
    César Manrique's museum **70**
  Las Palmas
    Canarian Museum 34
    Diocesan Museum of Sacred Arts 33
    Pueblo Canaria Museum 26
  La Palma
    Fine Arts Gallery 101
    Museum of Natural History and Ethnology 110
  Gran Canaria
    La Fortaleza Museum 49
    Piedras e Artesania Canaria Museum 44

Nelson, Horatio 11, 13, 87
Pájara, Fuerteventura 60, 61
Palacio de Carta bank, Tenerife 86, 88
paradores 16, 18, **14**

Parks
  Fuerteventura
    Dunes National Park 58
  Gran Canaria
    Arucas Municipal Park 46
    Palmitos Parque **9**
  La Gomera
    National Park of Garajonay 113, **114**, 115
  La Palma
    National Park of La Caldera de Taburiente 105
  Lanzarote
    Timanfaya National Park 5, **66**, 67; **71**
  Las Palmas
    Doramas Park **36**
    Parque San Telmo **35**
    Santa Catalina Park 37
  Tenerife
    Teide National Park 83, 92
Pérez Galdós Theatre 35
Plazas
  La Gomera
    Plaza Calvo Sotelo 116
  La Palma
    Plaza de Espa"na 102
  Las Palmas
    Plaza Santa Ana 33
  Tenerife
    Plaza Charco 92
    Plaza de España 85, 88
    Plaza de General Weyler **87**
    Plaza de la Candeleria 88
Pliny 68
pottery 29, **85**
Pueblo de Canario 31, 36
Puerto del Mogán 43, **44**
Puerto de Naos 99, **110**
Puerto del Rosario 55, 56
Puerto Rico **41**, 42
Reina Sofía International Airport 79, 85
Resorts
  Fuerteventura
    Caleta de Fueste 57,**59**
    Canada del Rio 62
    Costa Calma 62
    Los Goriones resort 62
    Matas Blancas resort 62
    Playa Esmeralda Jandía 62
    Playa Juan Gomez 62

Gran Canaria
  Arguineguín 43
  Maspolamas 41, 42, **43**
  Playa de Inglés 42
  San Augustín 42
Lanzarote
  Playa Blanca **5**, 56, **73**
  Puerto del Carmen **69**
Tenerife
  Costa del Silencio 83, 95
  Las Galletas 95
  Los Cristianos **83**, 95, 114
  Playa de las Américas 83, 85
  Puerto de la Cruz 88, 90
  Playa de Martianez 94
  Playa del Roque 89
Roque de Garachico 94
Roque del Este 78
Roque de los Muchachos 99, 104, 105
Roque del Oeste 78
Roque Nubio **48**
Roque Teneguia 110

San Antonio volcano 109
San Gabriel Fort **69**
San Marcos 88, 93
San Sebastián 115, **116**
Santa Maria **21**, 26, 101, 116
Santiago **119**

Taburiente crater 107
Teguise **75**, 76
Tejeda 48
Teneguia volcano 109
Tenerife 5, 6, **13**, 83, **93**
Torre del Conde **117**

Uga 72, 74

Valley of a Thousand Palms 77
Valley of La Aldea 45
Valley of Palms 60
Vegueta, Gran Canaria 43, 46
Vegueta Quarter, Las Palmas 5, 31, 33, 35, 37

Walsh, Bernard 85
watersports 22
windmills **61**
windsurfers **22**
wrestling 21, 73

Yaiza 71, 72
Ye 77